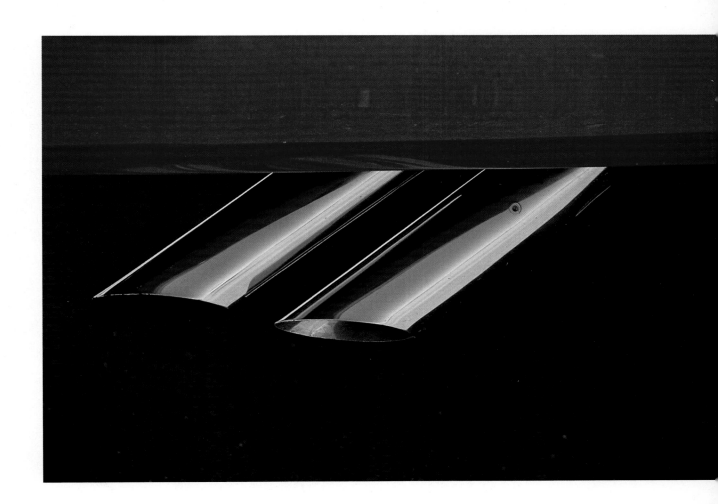

Motorbooks International

MUSCLE CAR COLOR HISTORY

GTO

1964–1967

Paul Zazarine

First published in 1991 by Motorbooks International Publishers & Wholesalers, PO Box 2, 729 Prospect Avenue, Osceola, WI 54020 USA

Motorbooks International books are also available at discounts in bulk quantity for industrial or sales-promotional use. For details write to Special Sales Manager at the Publisher's address

Library of Congress Cataloging-in-Publication Data
Zazarine, Paul.
    GTO 1964-1967 / Paul Zazarine.
        p.   cm. — (Motorbooks International muscle car color histories)
    Includes index.
    ISBN 0-87938-539-1
    1. GTO automobile.   I. Title.   II. Series.
TL215.G79Z39 1991
629.222'2—dc20   91-11014

Printed in Singapore by PH Productions

On the front cover: The license plate says it. This 1966 GTO was everything you could dream for.

On the back cover: The 1965 GTO convertible in Montero Red.

On the frontispiece: The trademark GTO exhaust splitters, an extra-cost option in 1964.

On the title page: The author's former 1966 GTO at speed.

Contents

Acknowledgments

During the course of writing this book on 1964–1967 GTOs, I was assisted by a number of friends whose help was instrumental in completing this project. Without sounding like an overdone Academy Award speech, I'd like to thank Donald Farr at Dobbs Publications for use of the *Musclecar Review* archives, Ed Lechtzin and Reg Harris at Pontiac Motor Division, Michael Dregni at Motorbooks and Greg Pernula for helping me find the ending. My love and thanks go especially to my wife, Nancy, who endures the long hours I spend in my office, pecking away at the word processor and emerging only briefly for food or sleep.

My thanks also to all the folks in the GTO hobby who allowed me to photograph their cars for this book, especially Bob Bassett, Jr., Richard Gill, John Truesdell, Eric White, Chuck Roberts, the late Bill Sherman, Milt Schornack, Dr. Stephen Bailey, Steve Brown, Bob Milloy and Ed Rowe.

Back in 1981, I spent over four hours interviewing Jim Wangers. The transcript runs 178 pages in length, and Jim covered just about every topic regarding Pontiac's performance history. You'll find excerpts from that interview interspersed throughout the book. But what intrigued me the most while rereading the interview in 1990 was Jim's concerns and opinions about the state of Pontiac's health back in the early 1980s. Pontiac had suffered through most of the 1970s with a lousy product mix and a tremendous lack of image, and by the early 1980s, the division was in damage control. All through the interview, Jim kept pounding away at what was wrong with Pontiac and what they needed to do to survive. "If they are not successful in reimaging that entire division around the new Trans Am," he told me, "I predict Pontiac is terminal." Jim then laid out the strategy he felt was needed to resurrect Pontiac and rebuild it into the performance division of General Motors.

During the interview ten years ago, as I listened to him talk about Pontiac's problems, I thought this was mostly a case of sour grapes. Jim wasn't in the loop at Pontiac anymore and, I assumed, he was frustrated because he could no longer bang on somebody's desk and get results like he had almost twenty years before.

Boy, was I wrong.

In 1983, Pontiac radically reimaged the division, and built a new reputation on performance with the Trans Am and sophistication with the STE. All of the things Jim had said Pontiac needed to do to survive had come to pass. There had been no sour grapes, and the frustration I had heard in his voice was there because he couldn't save the car company that he loved so much and had worked so hard for. It was only then that I realized Jim Wangers truly was an automotive marketing genius. Although he was part of a team at Pontiac that created some great cars, the GTO was Wangers' greatest achievement. Without his genius, his nurturing and his total devotion, the GTO would not have realized its destiny as America's premier musclecar.

This book is dedicated to him.

The package for 1964: license plate tag bracket from Royal Pontiac and a bolt-on set of Hurst wheels.

The Rise of Pontiac Performance

Long before Detroit had ever thought of a car like the Pontiac GTO, the movement toward high-performance automobiles was already under way. In the years preceding World War II, the birthplace of speed was in southern California. Young men whose names have become pillars of today's performance aftermarket industry—such as Edelbrock and Iskendarian—were modifying flathead Fords and building "rods" that exceeded the performance of even the most expensive production automobiles.

After the war, as Detroit produced cars to quench the thirst of a war-weary public, the word performance began creeping into the car maker's advertisements. The introduction of the high-compression Oldsmobile and Cadillac V–8 engines were the first shots fired in the horsepower wars that would escalate for more than two decades. In the early 1950s, Chrysler countered with the Hemi engine. Although displacing less than 350 ci at the time, the new Hemi was a boon to hot rodders and drag racers, who soon learned how to coax more power from it. Back in Detroit, product planners looked to the high-performance engines as a selling tool to attract buyers of large, luxurious models. The lower-priced models like Chevrolet, Plymouth and Pontiac had no V–8s. These cars were offered only with straight-sixes or straight-eight engines. They were sensible cars, and Detroit's perception was that sensible buyers wanted reliability and economy, not performance.

All of that changed in the fall of 1954 with the introduction of the 1955 models. The 1955 model year stands as a milestone for several reasons. A considerable number of car lines were restyled in 1955, marking more contemporary styling that appealed to the huge numbers of World War II veterans who were now in their mid- to late-thirties and growing more affluent. They could afford new cars, and they flooded dealer showrooms in droves. The industry set new sales records in 1955 thanks in part to the exciting new styling that appeared on Ford, GM and Chrysler products.

There was another, more significant revolution going on in 1955—the emergence of performance in the low-priced field. For the first time, Chevrolet and Pontiac offered V–8 engines. The small-block Chevrolet engine went on to become the cornerstone of street performance, and those southern California hot rodders who had built their passion for speed into profitable aftermarket parts businesses recognized the small-block Chevy as a gold mine of opportunity. Within a few years, a plethora of parts was offered to modify the Chevy Mouse Motor. New performance components are still being introduced today, nearly four decades after the 1955 model year.

While Pontiac's new V–8 didn't draw attention like Chevrolet's, it was a significant break from the past for a company that possessed a staid image of reliable

Call it the Wide Track Tiger, call it the Goat, call it The Great One—the GTO gave a new name to Pontiac as a performance automobile maker. It also revived Pontiac at a time when the future looked dim. By 1967, when this car was built, the GTO was at the top.

It's The Talk of the Test Drivers!

THE FABULOUS '56 PONTIAC WITH A BIG AND VITAL GENERAL MOTORS "AUTOMOTIVE FIRST"!

Believe us—it isn't easy to impress a test driver!

But they're cheering Pontiac in a big way.

What's set them buzzing is that big and vital General Motors "First" combining:

Pontiac's new big-bore Strato-Streak V-8 with the terrific thrust of 227 horsepower.

General Motors' new Strato-Flight Hydra-Matic* that gentles this mighty "go" to smoothness beyond belief.

You don't need a test track to prove that here is the lift of a lifetime.

Traffic tells you. Here's "stop-and-go" response as fast as thought itself. *A hill helps.* High or low, it's left behind without a sign of effort. *And passing definitely pins it down.* Gun it and in-stant, flashing power sweeps you swiftly by the loitering car ahead. No drag, no lag—just safe and certain "go"!

There's plenty more to charm you. The safety of big new brakes, a steady ride, advanced controls. Glamorous new beauty.

But, above all, it's that fabulous new "go" that gets you!

Drive a Pontiac today for a glorious double thrill. There'll be pride in your heart, a torrent at your toe-tip. What more could anyone want?

*An extra cost option.

'56 PONTIAC

PONTIAC MOTOR DIVISION OF GENERAL MOTORS CORPORATION

The new overhead Pontiac V–8 was introduced in 1955, replacing the straight-six and straight-eight engines that had powered Pontiacs since 1926. Introduced at 287 ci, it was enlarged to 316 ci in 1956, 347 ci in 1957, 370 ci in 1958 and 389 ci in 1959. It forever changed Pontiac's image and its fortunes.

The "torrent in your toe-tip" advertising embellishment may have been hyperbole in 1956, but it did signal the emergence of high performance at Pontiac, not only in the product itself, but in the advertising image presented to the public. The top of the line was the NASCAR engine, introduced in January 1956 with dual four-barrel carburetors and rated at a sizzling 285 hp.

yet boring transportation. In fact, sales had been so soft for so long that General Motors management had at one time considered slowly killing off the product by merging Pontiac with Oldsmobile, allowing the dealer body to either switch to Olds franchises when possible or simply closing them down.

Instead, a commitment was made to resuscitate Pontiac, and a changing of the guard was made in 1956. Semon "Bunkie" Knudsen, whose father had been with Pontiac two decades before, was moved into the office of general manager on July 1, 1956, and told to turn things around or possibly go down as the

last general manager the Pontiac Division would ever have. Knudsen went right to work. His first step was to evaluate Pontiac's product line-up and the perceived image of those products by the buying public. To increase sales and improve market penetration, Knudsen knew he had to turn his back on thirty years of image and build a new look. Younger customers were the target, and if Knudsen could win these buyers, the future belonged to Pontiac.

Within the first ninety days of his reign, Knudsen had stripped the chrome "suspenders" from the hood of the 1957 models, which were about to go into production. These chrome stripes were

By 1962, Pontiac ruled the high-back tracks of NASCAR, with drivers like Fireball Roberts and Joe Weatherly piloting the Smokey Yunick-prepared 421 ci Super Duty Catalinas. Pontiac General Manager Bunky Knudsen was a firm believer that "racing on Sunday and selling on Monday" was one of the keys to Pontiac's success in rising to the number-three sales slot behind Chevrolet and Ford.

legendary Tri-Power carburetion setup of three two-barrel carburetors. It also pumped up the horsepower and displacement of its engines and cleaned house at Daytona's 1957 Speed Week and NASCAR events. Knudsen personally directed the stock-car and drag-racing programs at Pontiac, searching out the best builders and tuners. Pontiac's blitzkrieg paid off, dominating stock-car racing and gathering the attention of the automotive press, which reported to enthusiasts that "Grandma's car" was now the hottest ticket going.

The successes enjoyed by Pontiac on the racetrack were paying dividends in the showroom as well. The introduction of the Wide Track Pontiacs in 1959 set the cars apart from the rest of the industry. These Hot Chiefs with their new engines were developing a reputation for performance that rubbed off on even the most mundane members of the Pontiac product line-up. By 1959, Pontiac had moved into the number-four spot behind Chevrolet, Ford and Plymouth, up from sixth place just four years before.

Knudsen had also influenced the styling of Pontiac. The first models under his direction debuted in 1959, and by 1963, Pontiac styling had broken new ground by using clean lines, an absence of excessive chrome trim and flaring the rear quarter panels. These styling cues would be picked up by every other manufacturer during the 1960s.

For his efforts, Knudsen was rewarded the top post at Chevrolet in 1961, and Estes moved into the general manager's chair. DeLorean was appointed chief engineer. The agenda for Pontiac set by Knudsen was accelerated by his successors. By 1962, Pontiac and its new line-up of Super Duty engines were literally ruling the racetracks and drag strips of America. Out of the ivy-covered walls of the Pontiac Engineering building emerged radical camshafts, aluminum exhaust headers, special lightweight aluminum body components, and lightened frames and wheels. Many of these parts were also offered for street applications, and the major performance magazines were now featuring articles and covers on the hot Pontiacs.

By this time, Wangers, DeLorean, Estes and others within Pontiac were riding the crest of a successful wave that had carried the division to the number-three

a throwback to the Silver Streaks that his father had been involved with at Pontiac in the early 1930s. Removing the chrome was more than a styling ploy; it broke the bond with tradition and paved the way for new interpretations of what Pontiac signified as a car maker.

Knudsen also hired a group of young engineers to fulfill his vision for a new Pontiac. He had determined that for Pontiac to succeed, it had to cash in on the success the industry had enjoyed in 1955. The excitement of performance, of youthful styling that was a departure from the heavy, bulbous lines of the past, couldn't be understood by men who clung to high collars and French-tip shoes. In September 1956, Knudsen hired Elliot "Pete" Estes as chief engineer. Estes had been involved in the design of the high-compression Olds V-8 and favored high performance. Knudsen also brought aboard a bright young engineer from Packard, John Z.

DeLorean, to become director of Advanced Engineering.

Soon the word was out that things were happening at Pontiac, and that attracted more young engineers, product planners and designers. It also attracted a young man named Jim Wangers who had some unique ideas about how to image and sell cars. Wangers had been at Campbell-Ewald, Chevrolet's advertising agency, and was instrumental in the campaign to change Chevy's image in 1955 by emphasizing performance. After a short stint at Chrysler, Wangers was recruited by McManus, John and Adams, Pontiac's advertising agency.

Within eighteen months of Knudsen's arrival, a barrage of high-performance packages and programs began to hit the automotive world. Thanks to Estes, who brought the concept of multiple carburetion with him from Oldsmobile, Pontiac introduced in 1957 the now-

A harbinger of things to come was the 1963 Tempest, dressed out for road-racing or drag-strip action. Equipped with the Super Duty 421 ci engine but still using the stock rear transaxle and "rope" driveshaft, these Super Tempests paved the way for what would eventually become the GTO.

sales position. Wangers was finely attuned to the street scene, and he reported to DeLorean what the emerg-

ing generation of gearheads was doing and how he thought Pontiac could be a part of it. Wangers met George Hurst and introduced him to the engineers at Pontiac. Soon Pontiac became the first car maker to use Hurst's new floorshifter. Virtually everyone on the street was converting to Hursts, and Pontiac's adaptation of the stout stick was an indication of just how much in touch Pontiac—and Wangers—was with the high-performance scene.

Pontiac was on an incredible roll, with huge successes on the tracks, a *Motor Trend* Car of the Year Award under its belt and a hot performance image that staked its booming showroom sales to continued dominance on the tracks. They were the envy of the industry, and just when it appeared nothing could go wrong, Pontiac was dealt a blow that threatened to crumble the dynasty Knudsen and his successors had so carefully built.

1964 GTO

The Instant Performance Automobile

Pontiac had hitched its image to performance, and while they still built four-cylinder Tempests and nine-passenger Safari station wagons, the aura of Super Duties and Tri-Power Bonnevilles rubbed off on even the most mundane cars in the product line-up. The success of these pavement-melting Pontiacs was directly related to the division's domination on the tracks. In NASCAR, Fireball Roberts and Joe Weatherly had piloted Pontiacs to the winner's circle before tens of thousands of rabid car enthusiasts. On the NHRA drag strips, Jim Wangers' victory in Stock Eliminator at the 1960 NHRA Nationals drew considerable attention from the automotive press. The emerging popularity of Super Stock racing showcased the power of the 389 ci, followed by the 421 ci Super Duty Pontiac engines and drivers like Arnie Beswick, Arlen Vanke and Hayden Profitt.

The racing and performance image carefully cultivated by Pontiac was suddenly threatened by the January 24,

The GTO hardtop featured clean and functional styling that looked great from any angle.

1963, GM corporate edict that specified Pontiac and sister division Chevrolet absolve themselves from all racing activities. Any backdoor support of other racing teams carrying the division banner was also to be terminated. With one stroke of the corporate pen, the careful work of five years had just been torpedoed by GM management.

History records success as the convergence of luck and timing, and both of these factors played a part in the birth of the GTO. Ever since the Tempest had arrived in 1961 with its four-cylinder engine derived by splitting the Pontiac V-8 in half, "rope" driveshaft and rear transaxle, the idea of dropping a 389 into the engine bay had been discussed. A handful of 421 powered Tempests had been built in 1963 for drag racing in the Factory Experimental class; however, these cars still utilized the rear transaxle, and were never considered for production. The year before, Pontiac Engineering had even gone as far as submitting an application to the FIA (the international racing federation) for a 389 ci powered Tempest to go road racing.

General Motors planned to abandon the radical drivetrain layout for the Tempest in the 1964, reverting back to a

For the man who wouldn't mind riding a tiger if someone'd only put wheels on it—Pontiac GTO

This piece of machinery is something our Engineering Department slipped a motherly big Pontiac 389-incher into and named the GTO.

It comes in hardtop, sports coupe and convertible form, based on the Le Mans—only sleekened down some and fitted with a special set of red-circle high-performance tires.

The looks you can see for yourself. The big deal is under the hood: 325 bhp at 4800 rpm and 428 lb-ft of torque at 3200 rpm. That's just the standard 4BBL engine. There's also a version with 348 bhp* at 4900 rpm and 428 lb-ft of torque at 3600 rpm. *optional at extra cost.

This one does deep-breathing exercises through a 3-2BBL setup. Both make bad-tempered noises through dual pipes. As illustrated above, pairs of exhaust splitters on each flank, just behind the rear wheels, are available dealer installed*.

A 3-speed transmission is standard, stirred by a Hurst shifter on the floor. Extra-cost variations include an automatic with shift on the column . . . an all-synchro 4-speed on the floor . . . or a choice of any one of them sprouting out of a console.

Give yourself a blast of tonic. Sample one of these here big pussycats.

PONTIAC MOTOR DIVISON • GENERAL MOTORS CORPORATION

16

standard drivetrain, powered by a base six-cylinder with the 326 ci engine as an option. Since the 326 and 389 engines shared the same exterior dimensions and used the same motor mounts, Pontiac Engineering began experimenting with a 389 powered 1963 Tempest, simply as an engineering experiment. The work of Pontiac engineers Bill Collins and John DeLorean couldn't have come at a better time. While their project was simply an experiment, they had unknowingly laid the groundwork for a Super Tempest. DeLorean already had a name for it—GTO.

It was Wangers' vision that solidified the creation of the GTO, based on the engineering experiments. Wangers recognized Pontiac would have to transfer its performance image from the racetrack and put it on the street, thanks to GM's ban on racing. He also saw the budding "youth market" that he believed would snap up a low-priced car that was the antithesis of what its parents drove. Make it affordable, give it flash, give it image and give it the powertrain to blow away virtually any car on the street. As he had in the past, Wangers passed his idea on to DeLorean of dropping the big Pontiac 389 engine into the new Tempest and turning it loose on the streets. It was the recipe for success, and DeLorean recognized it instantly. The engineering experiment was on its way to becoming a production reality.

While the concept of slipping a big engine under a small hood sounds simple enough, no car maker had ever seriously attempted to bring the combination to production. The Pontiac team had one other obstacle—a GM edict that restricted engine displacement and horsepower output in mid-sized cars. That wasn't all. Any new models had to have the approval of the corporation, and a car that didn't meet corporate guidelines didn't stand a chance of getting the GM nod. DeLorean and Wangers realized *options* were not subject to approval. They also knew it was easier to ask forgiveness than permission, so a concentrated team effort was made to

A device for shrinking time and distance
Pontiac GTO

The 1964 GTO brochure was straightforward about what the GTO was all about. "To be perfectly honest," Pontiac warned, "the GTO is not everyone's cup of tea. Designed as a piece of performance machinery, its purpose in life is to permit you to make the most of your driving skill. Its suspension is firm, tuned more to the open road than to wafting gently over bumpy streets. Its dual exhausts won't win any prizes for whispering. And, unless you order it with our lazy 3.08 low-ratio rear axle, its gas economy won't be anything to write home about. If all this dismays you, then you're almost certainly a candidate for one of our 27 other Pontiac Pontiacs and Pontiac Tempests. But if you're tuned in to our particular wave length, if you start vibrating when you're at the controls of a sudden automobile, if you've driven enough different kinds of performance to know what it's all about, then you've got GTO written right across your forehead."

Pontiac had led the way with clean styling and sparse use of chrome beginning with the

1963 Grand Prix. The 1964 GTO continued that tradition.

Unlike most other high-performance cars of the time, the GTO's office was luxurious, with door-to-door carpeting, plush seats and aluminum-turned applique on the instrument panel.

Previous page
One of three body styles was the sport coupe. The bright trim around the windows and wheel openings on this Singapore Gold 1964 was standard as part of the LeMans package, from which the GTO option was ordered.

Next page
The standard GTO engine displaced 389 ci and utilized a single Carter AFB four-barrel carburetor. It was rated at 325 hp.

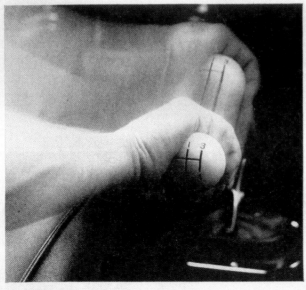

GTO is for kicking up the kind of storm that others just talk up.

Standard Equipment: engine: 389-cu. in. Pontiac with 1-4BBL; bhp—325 @ 4800; torque—428 lb-ft @ 3200 rpm/dual-exhaust system/3-speed stick with Hurst shifter/heavy-duty clutch/heavy-duty springs, shocks, stabilizer bar/special 7.50 x 14 red-line high-speed nylon cord tires (rayon cord whitewalls optional at no extra cost)/14 x 6JK wide-rim wheels/high-capacity radiator / declutching fan / high-capacity battery (66 plate, 61 amp. hr.)/chromed air cleaner, rocker covers, oil filler cap/bucket seats/standard axle ratio 3.23:1 (3.08, 3.36*, 3.55* to 1 available on special order at no extra cost). **And some of our extra-cost Performance Options:** engine: 389-cu. in. Pontiac with 3-2BBL (Code #809); bhp—348 @ 4900;

Available only with heavy-duty options at slight additional charge.

torque—428 lb-ft @ 3600; 3.55:1 axle ratio standard with this engine option/4-speed with Hurst shifter (gear ratios 2.56:1, 1.91:1, 1.48:1, 1.00:1, and 2.64:1 reverse)/2-speed automatic with 2.20:1 torque converter/Safe-T-Track limited-slip differential (Code #701)/3.90:1 axle ratio available on special order with metallic brake linings, heavy-duty radiator and Safe-T-Track/handling kit—20:1 quick steering and extra-firm-control heavy-duty shocks (Code #612)/high-performance full transistor (breakerless) ignition (Code #671)/tachometer (Code #452)/custom sports steering wheel (Code #524)/exhaust splitters (Dealer installed)/wire wheel discs (Dealer installed)/custom wheel discs, with spinner and brake cooling holes (Code #521)/console (Code #601).

the GTO makers—Pontiac

PONTIAC MOTOR DIVISION • GENERAL MOTORS CORPORATION

The GTO hardtop was released in November 1963. This Grenadier Red 1964 is fitted with Custom wheel covers. Exhaust splitters were an extra-cost option. Instead of the standard exhaust pipe exiting under the rear bumper, the splitters located the exhaust behind the rear wheel openings.

Previous page
This ad is what Wangers called "selling the sizzle with the steak." By listing all the options available for the GTO, no other copy was necessary. The GTO sold itself to a performance-starved America.

get the GTO off the ground as an option on the LeMans.

There was only one other hurdle before the GTO could become reality: it had to be sold to Pontiac management. Regardless of how excited Wangers and DeLorean were about the car, without the backing of Pontiac management, the idea of a high-performance street car would remain just that—a dream.

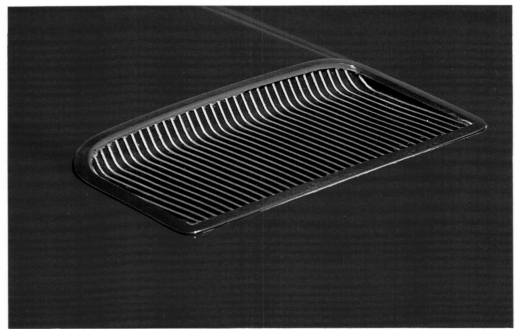

One of the cues that identified the GTO from the LeMans was the twin chromed scoops located on either side of the hood. The pot-metal scoop ornaments were nonfunctional.

While the Hurst floorshifter was standard on all three- and four-speed transmission GTOs, the center console was an extra-cost option.

Previous page
This Silvermist Gray sport coupe is owned by Pontiac Motor Division and is part of the Pontiac Historical Collection. It is equipped with the base 325 hp engine and four-speed transmission.

The GTO's savior would be in the form of Elliot "Pete" Estes, successor to Knudsen as general manager of Pontiac Motor Division. Estes was an engineer and a "car guy." If he could be sold, and if he had the courage to stand up to the corporation once the car was slipped into the hands of the dealer body, the GTO was assured of success. Without his support, it would never see the light of day.

A power top was standard on GTO convertibles. Wire wheel covers were optional.

*The GTO Tri-Power was vacuum operated;
however, most owners removed the vacuum
setup and switched to a mechanical linkage
that responded faster to throttle position.*

*Previous page
The optional engine also displaced 389 ci and
was rated at 348 hp. It utilized Pontiac's
legendary Tri-Power—three Rochester two-
barrel carburetors.*

To his credit, Estes stood behind the
young Pontiac engineers and the vision-
ary advertising executive. Estes over-
came the objections of the sales management team, a group of Pontiac
executives entrenched in methods they
had used to sell cars since the 1940s.
They were certain the car would never
sell; dealers would end up eating this
colossal failure. The confrontation between the young lions and the old veterans nearly led to fisticuffs, but in the end,
Estes pushed the car through the division and to the dealers. The history
books will record he was truly the
unsung hero of the Pontiac GTO.

Selling the 1964 GTO to a perfor-
mance-hungry America was no prob-
lem. In fact, Pontiac's strategy at first was
to introduce the car with a low-key
approach, just in case it wasn't the sure-
fire success Wangers and DeLorean believed it to be. "Once the car was out

into the hands of the dealers," Wangers
recalled, "there was no way the corporation was going to break it down and
make the General Manager look bad in
the eyes of the dealers."

By January, dealers were taking orders
for the GTO, and by the end of the
model year, 32,450 copies were roaming
the streets, making boulevard fodder of
nearly everything on wheels. For the first
time, anyone's Walter Mitty fantasies
could be fulfilled by simply walking into
a Pontiac dealer, plunking down three
grand and driving away in a car that was
virtually unbeatable.

What was a GTO, and what did it have
that no other car offered? While the
GTO was essentially a LeMans, sitting on
a 115 in. wheelbase, it was a *package*.
Checking off the W62 GTO option delivered a 389 ci engine, replacing the
LeMans' 326 ci powerplant. It was topped
by a Carter AFB four-barrel carburetor,
the high-compression heads from the
big 421 ci engine and a moderate-lift
hydraulic camshaft. The camshaft used a
duration of 273 degrees on intake and
289 degrees on exhaust. Lift measured
0.400 in. for intake and 0.410 in. for
exhaust. The package was good for 325
hp at 4800 rpm. A chromed air cleaner
and valve covers added visual excitement to an already visceral engine.

In standard form, along with the 325
hp 389, the GTO was equipped with a
three-speed manual gearbox and Hurst

calling all sports car enthusiasts!

Grab This — For Size! Pontiac's All-New

CUSTOM SPORTS STEERING WHEEL

(CODE 524)

Here's a wheel with that rugged sports car flair, combined with distinctive good looks! Handsome, wood-grain styled steering wheel (finger grips all around) . . . bold, stainless steel spokes . . . center horn button. Complements the walnut instrument panel inserts of any Bonneville or Grand Prix interior . . . just "purr-fect" with a 2 + 2 or G.T.O. option. **Available All 7 Pontiac Series—Factory-Installed Only!**

Suggested Retail Price

$43.04	20 exc. w/Decor
$39.27	(20 with 064) 21-22
$43.04	23 exc. w/Decor or 2 + 2 Sports Option
$28.52	26-28-29 & 23 w/Decor or 2 + 2 Sports Option

The handsome GTO instrument panel was devoid of gauges save for the fuel gauge and speedometer. The only available gauge was a tachometer, located in the far right-hand pod.

Previous page
The Custom Sport wheel looked like wood but wasn't, felt like wood but didn't splinter like wood. Every GTO from 1964 to 1970 could be equipped with a wood-like sport wheel; however, the 1964 was the only four-spoke design.

floorshifter, dual exhausts, GTO emblems on the quarters, trunk lid and front fenders, as well as two chromed, nonfunctional hood scoops. Below deck, the GTO boasted stiffer springs and shocks and a larger front antisway bar. If there was one drawback to the GTO, it was the brakes; they were the same 9.5 in. drums as used with the six-cylinder Tempest. They were admittedly inferior for the tremendous power the GTO possessed under the hood. Ordering the optional metallic linings made a consid-

The woodgrained, four-spoke Custom Sport steering wheel was optional. The horn button was adorned by the Pontiac crest.

The GTO nameplate also appeared on the rear quarter panels. A smaller version of the nameplate was affixed to the rear deck lid.

erable difference in the GTO's stopping power, however. The hotter they got, the better they would work, with little fade.

The legendary Tri-Power was optional for the GTO, with its three Rochester two-barrel carbs and vacuum-controlled linkage. Normal operation was with the center two-holer, but at approximately seventy-percent throttle the two outer carbs would open and produce a banshee-like wail as the 389 wound out to produce 348 hp at 4900 rpm. Under wide-open throttle, the GTO accelerated like a rocket. The driver held on to the wheel and it was all he could do to remember to watch the tach and power-shift through the gears.

Wrapped in a lightweight body, even in its most mild-mannered form, the GTO could streak down the quarter mile in the high-fourteens. A Tri-Power version, hooked to the Muncie close-ratio four-speed transmission and 3.90:1 rear axle, could clear the traps in the high-thirteens at a top speed of 108 mph. The 0–60 mph time was in the vicinity of five seconds. There wasn't another car selling at that price that could equal those figures.

The optional 7000 rpm tachometer was located in the far right-hand instrument panel pod. The gauge was rather small and difficult to see.

While the GTO was affordable, it wasn't Spartan. The interior was luxurious for a mid-sized car, with door-to-door carpeting, plush seats, an aluminum-turned dash applique and the unique GTO emblem above the glovebox door. What made the GTO even more exciting was Pontiac's option list, which according to Pontiac Motor Division, was "as long as your arm and twice

Buying the Ultimate 1964 GTO

Imagine for a moment it's 1964, and you've walked into a Pontiac dealer to order a GTO. On the showroom is a Cameo Ivory convertible, but it's equipped with the four-barrel engine and automatic transmission. On the lot are a few other GTOs, all four-barrels, a few with four-speeds, and the salesman tries in vain to push one of these milquetoast models. You refuse, because you know exactly how you want your dream GTO to be dressed out—Grenadier Red with a black interior. You instruct the salesman to break out the order form and you go to work:

Code	Description	Price
2237	LeMans Hardtop Sport Coupe	$2,556.00
382	Gran Turismo Omologato	295.90
393	Radio—Push Button & Electric Antenna	92.16
404	Lamp, Underhood	3.55
421	Washer & Wipers—W/S	17.27
422	Extensions—Tail Pipe	21.30
452	Tachometer	53.80
471	Lamps—Back-up	12.91
474	Rear Speaker—VerbaPhonic	53.80
501	Power Steering	96.84
502	Power Brakes	42.50
524	Steering Wheel—Custom Sports	39.27
601	Console	48.15
621	Springs—Heavy Duty	3.82
701	Differential—Safe-T-Track	37.66
661	Frame—Heavy Duty	23.35
809	389 V-8 3/2BBL	115.78
009	Transmission—Four-Speed Syncromesh	188.30
Total Price		$3,702.36

You also specified the 3.90 rear axle, since you plan to enter the stock class at the drag strip. After some haggling, the dealer gives you $700 for your 1960 Chevrolet Impala trade-in. You also have a grand in cash for a down payment, leaving a balance of $2,000 to finance for thirty-six months. You can easily handle the payments of $65 per month.

The deal and your credit are approved, and after six long weeks of waiting, your GTO rolls off the hauler at the dealer. After prep and filling out the paperwork, you take the GTO out and start looking for pigeons driving Chevys.

It didn't take long for this emblem to earn a reputation on the street. Most street racers knew better than to tangle with a GTO. "If you don't think this is enough warning," Pontiac noted, "you could always fly the skull and crossbones."

Previous page
The LeMans grille was blacked out and the GTO nameplate was installed.

as hairy." Judicious use of the order book could build a car for high-speed luxury cruising or for just blowing the hubcaps off the competition on the street. Options included air conditioning, a handsome four-spoke "wood" wheel (actually constructed of plastic), tachometer and several radio choices.

The beauty of the GTO was, like the big Pontiac models, the customer could option out a GTO to suit his preferences. A buyer who was strictly performance-minded checked off the high-performance options to package his GTO for drag racing, where the GTO would dominate the B/Stock classes. For those buyers who wanted the boulevard image of driving a GTO but desired creature comforts, there was a plethora of luxury options ranging from power windows to

a power antenna. The ultimate GTO was a combination of all these options. It was possible to literally build a poor-man's Grand Prix from the GTO option list.

The GTO hit the streets and instantly gained recognition as *the* high-performance car. In Detroit, no other manufacturer was prepared to compete against the GTO until the 1964 model year was virtually over. Oldsmobile fielded the 4-4-2, a competent package but underpowered with its 330 ci V-8. Buick assembled the Gran Sport Skylark by dropping in its 401 engine, but Buick lacked the performance image of Pontiac and sales were far behind the GTO. Although Chevrolet had its potent 409 engine, the Chevelle SS still relied on the 327 small-block; however, it was given a shot in the arm by offering the 350 hp Corvette 327. But it wasn't a big-cube engine, and that was part of the GTO's success.

The other car makers were slow to offer alternatives in 1964. Dodge and Plymouth were building special lightweight full-sized cars, but they were limited in production and quite expensive. They were also purpose-built as race cars, and as such were difficult to maintain and their drivability didn't match the GTO. Ford's Fairlane qualified

It didn't take long for GTOs to hit the drag strips, competing and winning in B/Stock. The Pampered Papoose *driven by Howard Maseles was sponsored by Packer Pontiac.*

Optional at extra cost was a manifold vacuum gauge mounted on the center console. It was available with manual or automatic transmissions.

as a mid-sized car, but the hottest engine offered was the code K 271 hp 289 ci engine. The top performance engine in the new Mustang was the 225 hp 289. The days of high-horsepower pony cars were still a few years away.

To indicate just how good a package the GTO could be, *Car and Driver* made a comparison of the GTO to its namesake, the Ferrari GTO. Using two GTOs prepared by Royal Pontiac, Pontiac's

The chrome-flashed Deluxe wheel cover was optional and featured ten cooling slots surrounding the center ornament. The 7.50x14 in. US Royal Tiger Paws were standard on all 1964 GTOs.

The Custom wheel cover was a three-piece affair with eight cooling slots in the wheel cover, a retaining band and a diecast, three-ear spinner ornament.

backdoor performance dealer in Royal Oak, Michigan, *Car and Driver* wrote that in their opinion the Pontiac GTO did everything the Ferrari could do for a lot less money. "We made a very bold statement with that story," Jim Wangers recalled. "Here we took the darling of the sports car set, the Ferrari, and put it up against something as gauche as a Pon-

tiac. The whole thing was just great image-building press for Pontiac."

The GTO captured the imagination of America. Although overshadowed by the fabulous Mustang, the introduction of the 1964 GTO opened the door for affordable performance. It appealed to the very market Wangers was in touch with: young buyers who wanted the looks and image the GTO provided. The GTO became much like the Corvette in that it was a rolling personal statement.

The tremendous success achieved by the GTO also meant Wangers' vision had been correct. The GTO carried out its mission, transferring Pontiac's image from the racetrack to the street. Its future and the continued strength of Pontiac as a builder of high-performance cars was ensured.

The fuel filler door was located in the center of the taillamp panel, which was trimmed in Marimba Red.

GTO interiors were offered in either Black, Dark Blue, Light Saddle, Dark Aqua, Medium Red or the Parchment scheme shown here with Custom Sport steering wheel. A variation of the fender emblem appeared on the instrument panel just above the glovebox door.

Royal Pontiac

The Performance Dealership

The story of Royal Pontiac reaches back to the late 1950s, when Ace Wilson, Jr., purchased a Pontiac franchise in Royal Oak, Michigan, a suburb on Woodward Avenue halfway between Detroit and Pontiac. Wilson's new Pontiac store was located on North Main Street, not far from Jim Wangers' home in Royal Oak.

Wangers, already established as an advocate of high performance, had been pushing for a network of Pontiac dealers across the country who would become performance dealers, specializing in sales and service of Pontiac Hot Chiefs. Wangers was turned down several times, but his persistence finally paid off. Frank Bridge, Pontiac's general sales manager, eventually agreed to allow Wangers to find one dealer who was willing to be a guinea pig. If the dealer would agree to stock special cars and special parts and get involved in special activities—read drag racing—Bridge promised to find a way of supporting it. The catch was, the connection

Of the two GTOs prepared by Royal for the Car and Driver *road test, only this Grenadier Red sport coupe survives.*

had to be covert. "I don't want anyone to know it," Bridge told Wangers.

Wangers hooked up with Wilson and things began to happen. "Wilson liked racing," Wangers recalled. "He liked performance, he was a relatively new Pontiac dealer and he thought this was a swinging idea."

Royal's switch to GTOs was complete by 1965, and they campaigned a pair of Bobcats across the Midwest and the East. The tiger theme was a natural tie-in with the Bobcat package, and Hurst was a major player in supplying shifters and wheels for the cars. Notice the driver in the foreground wearing a tiger suit.

Within six months, Royal established a reputation as the dealer that stocked the fastest cars, had the service technicians that knew how to work on them and a parts department stocked with an assortment of aftermarket and factory performance parts. Wangers took the Royal name before the national press in 1960 when he piloted *Hot Chief Number 1* to the Stock Eliminator title at the NHRA Nationals in Detroit.

Wilson realized the vast potential in the sales and service of high-performance Pontiacs. "In this day and age of professional drag strip racers," stated Royal's 1963 brochure, "car dealers who sponsor Super Stocks are a dime a dozen. At Royal Pontiac, there's a difference. Most dealers who sponsor these hot jobs at the drag strip are content to sit back and wait. They figure a winner or even reasonable success at the strip will mean that all the local enthusiasts will "knock down the doors" to do business at their dealership. This just doesn't happen. At Royal, we go a step further. A successful Super Stocker at the strip is only the beginning. We want to pass our

experience on to you. We want to satisfy your performance needs and problems. We are prepared to offer all the Pontiac factory options plus a custom performance tune-up that is guaranteed to outperform any equivalent Pontiac in showroom stock condition. This treatment is called the 'Royal Bobcat' tune-up package."

It was this philosophy that set Royal Pontiac apart from the mainstream of dealers who weren't versed in the performance market or were apprehensive about the profitability of racing, building and selling special high-performance cars. But racing was just part of the Royal story.

"One of the first things I convinced Ace Wilson to do was to package a car that incorporated some of the special services and the special parts that he was putting into these cars and that's how the Royal Bobcat was born," Wangers recalled. "The Bobcat was created in 1961 off of a Catalina, and it's funny how we arrived at the name Bobcat. Back in those days Pontiac was putting their nameplates on their cars in big, separate

letters with little holes drilled in the sheetmetal. They had model names like Catalina, Ventura and Bonneville. Out of the words Bonneville and Catalina, we came up with the name Bobcat and the letters fit into the same number of holes that Catalina did."

The Bobcat was a packaged performance car, utilizing many of the performance options offered by Pontiac. Starting with the 389 Tri-Power, Royal used the factory's free-flowing exhaust manifolds and dual exhausts, aluminum wheels with the integral drums, four-speed manual gearbox and limited-slip rear. Royal then made special modifications to the car to make it a Bobcat. The distributor curve was reworked, as were

40

Jim Wangers in his trademark white baseball cap checks his mirror while racing the 1962 Hot Chief. Wangers cleaned house in this car, with a best of 12.38 seconds at 116.23 mph. The beautiful red and gold Poncho weighed in at a svelte 3,600 lb., thanks to extensive use of factory lightweight aluminum body components. The 421 was shifted at 6000 rpm and cranked out over 450 hp. It was the most successful Pontiac Royal had ever built.

the carburetor jets. The vacuum carburetor linkage was scrapped for a mechanical setup, and less restrictive mufflers were installed.

To visually set the Bobcat apart, all Catalina nameplates were removed, special paint was applied and the Bobcat nameplate was installed. "It was the first, really packaged supercar," recalled Wangers.

Royal began taking cues from both Pontiac and the aftermarket, and by 1963 they were reworking camshaft timing,

The official membership decal of the Royal Racing Team. Additional decals were available for 50¢.

Previous page
Shrouded in controversy, the Royal Bobcat GTO that blew the collective minds of the sophisticated staff of Car and Driver *has been fingered as a ringer because of its stock-nonstock status. Insiders like Wangers will swear the GTO was equipped with the stock 389 engine. Others believe the 389 was pulled and the bruising 421 HO with over 376 hp installed.*

changing compression ratios and making adjustments to the valvetrain to increase rpm.

It was the emergence of the GTO that ended the short reign of the Bobcat. Much that Wangers had learned in building the Bobcat package he related to the GTO. "When Pontiac finally created the one symbol of what Pontiac was all about in a total package called the GTO, there wasn't any room for a Royal Bobcat. So the Royal Bobcat

The Royal Team toured the country, leaving Detroit on Friday nights and pulling back into town the following week. It was hard work, recalled Milt Schornack, especially when he had a pile of work to face after racing the GTOs all weekend. Royal received tremendous exposure, thanks to the racing team and the numerous magazine articles written about the Bobcat-equipped GTOs.

became a tuning package or a performance package for the GTO, the 2+2 and later the Firebird."

When the GTO arrived on the scene, Royal began experimenting with the GTO, using the tricks they had learned over the years to juice the big Pontiac engine. The distributors were recurved, thin head gaskets were installed to boost compression, the carburetors were rejetted and the lifters were restricted by installing special fiber lock nuts that reduced lifter pump-up and allowed another 500 rpm. This became the Royal Bobcat package, and it could be installed in a GTO by Royal, or shipped as a kit with all necessary parts and instructions for installation by the customer.

The Royal Bobcat package on a GTO was identified by a decal that was applied to the C-pillar. Pontiac fans were also urged to send $3 and join the Royal Racing Team. Membership included a special window decal, price sheets for parts and services and a newsletter. To own a GTO with the Bobcat package, a Royal Racing Team decal on the windshield and a Royal license plate frame was to be one of the "swingingest" dudes on the street.

With the urging of Wangers, who was a "consultant" to Royal, the top car

The Car and Driver 1964 GTO launches with Milt Schornack at the wheel. The late Bill Sherman, who had owned the GTO since late 1964, brought the car out of storage several years ago with the help of Schornack. Schornack once campaigned the GTO at nostalgic drag-racing events across the country.

The Mystery Driver wearing the tiger suit would appear everywhere the Royal Racing Team went. Spectators were urged to race the Mystery Tiger and try to beat him in one of the Royal GTOs. The Mystery Tiger promotion came to a close when the costume was doffed to reveal George Hurst himself, although Hurst didn't always play the part.

CAR and DRIVER

MARCH 1964 · 50 CENTS

Tempest GTO: 0-to-100 in 11.8 sec
Who Killed Studebaker? – Page 75
Rover 2000 Road Research Report

When the "GTO vs. GTO" article appeared in the March 1964 issue of Car and Driver, it created a storm of controversy. In the magazine's opinion, the Pontiac GTO was easily the equal of the Ferrari GTO. After the maga- zine hit the stands in late January 1964, GTO sales began to skyrocket. Editor David E. Davis still believes the article guaranteed the success of both the GTO and Car and Driver.

magazines like *Hot Rod*, *Car Craft* and *Super Stock* beat a path to Royal to road test Bobcat GTOs and write articles on how Milt Schornack could supertune the GTO engine for more power and faster acceleration. It was not unusual to see pictures of Schornack bent over a Sun distributor, carefully setting the advance curve, or Royal mechanic Dave Warren cracking gears on the drag strip.

Because of the success of Royal Pontiac, there was considerable communication between Schornack and Pontiac Engineering. Parts would travel back and forth, and Schornack would experiment with setups and report back to Engineering on the results. One of the earliest experiments conducted by Royal that eventually appeared in production GTOs was cold-air induction, which Pontiac named Ram Air. Ram Air was introduced as an accessory package in 1965 after Royal had perfected the setup on the 1964 and 1965 GTOs.

Ace Wilson sold the performance arm of the dealership in 1969 to George (brother of John Z.) DeLorean's Leader Automotive. Royal Pontiac was eventually sold by Wilson, and a special era in Pontiac performance was over.

Milt Schornack nails second gear in a 1966 Royal Bobcat GTO. Schornack worked closely with many national magazines, preparing cars and doing the driving at local tracks like Motor City and Ubly. One of the most successful promotions was the GeeTO Tiger that appeared on the cover of the December 1965 issue of Car Craft.

Every Royal-equipped GTO received this decal, which was placed on the C-pillar of 1964 models. Later on, the decal could be ordered through the mail, and many a GTO that was neither a Bobcat nor which had been purchased from Royal wore this badge of honor.

Milt Schornack behind the wheel of the Car and Driver *Royal Bobcat GTO. Since the car was uncovered several years ago, Schornack has driven and displayed the GTO at shows across the country. He has retained much of the car's original appearance; however, it runs much stronger than it did on the street in 1964.*

The Mysterious *Car and Driver* Royal Bobcat

Perhaps one of the most famous Royal Bobcats was this Grenadier Red 1964, built on November 2, 1963, and eventually shipped to Royal on November 8. What happened to the car during that six-day period is open for conjecture; however, it most likely spent a few days next door at the Pontiac Engineering garage before finding its way to Royal Oak. Equipped with the 348 hp Tri-Power and four-speed transmission, the GTO was given the "Royal Treatment" and then delivered to Jim Wangers, who turned it—and an identical GTO painted blue—over to *Car and Driver* magazine. *Car and Driver* wrung both cars out at Daytona, spinning a rod in the red car and using the blue one for the remainder of the tests.

The Royal Bobcat GTOs accelerated from 0–60 mph in 4.6 seconds and turned the quarter mile in the low-thirteens. *Car and Driver* made no bones that the cars were tweaked by Royal, and pronounced the Pontiac GTO to be the equal of its Ferrari namesake in its March 1964 issue, which elicited howls of protest from the magazine's European-oriented readers, but provided Pontiac with reams of copy and great PR. It was after the *Car and Driver* test that GTO sales went ballistic.

What has remained a bone of contention to this day is what happened to the two GTOs during their stay at Pontiac Engineering. Some who were involved in servicing or driving the cars after they returned from Florida swear the two were equipped not with 389s but the thumping 421 HO (High Output), a behemoth that delivered 370 hp and was virtually impossible to distinguish from a 389.

The blue GTO was allegedly destroyed in a fire some years ago. The red car remains, and is now in the hands of Milt Schornack, who became the wizard of Royal in the mid-1960s, not long after the Grenadier Red 1964 GTO had made its triumphant return from road-test immortality. Schornack once campaigned the GTO at nostalgia drag races, turning low-elevens thanks to a vintage 421 HO and modified suspension.

The Car and Driver *Royal Bobcat* is today equipped with a 421 HO engine. Rumors continue to fly as to whether the GTO tested by Car and Driver *was a ringer or legitimately powered by a stock 389 with Royal supertuning.*

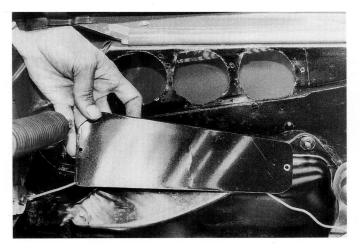

Royal used the 1964 Bobcat for various performance experiments, including a cold-air induction system that utilized three tubes fitted from the firewall above the heater box routed to a specially modified air cleaner. A plate now covers the holes Schornack cut over a quarter century ago.

Schornack installed a vintage Sun tach and underhood gauges for drag racing. The Bobcat was campaigned locally for several months after its road test in Florida for Car and Driver.

1965 GTO

America Discovers the Tiger

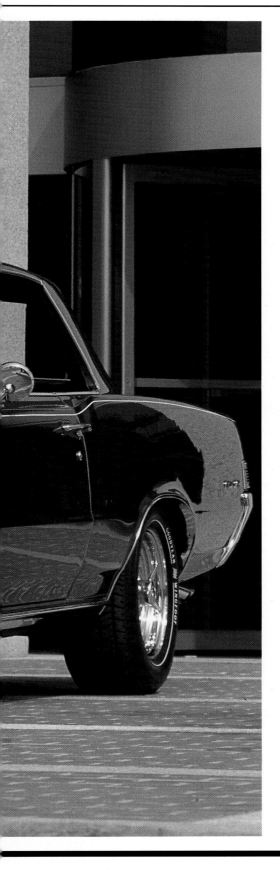

When Humble Oil began their ad campaign in 1962 urging Americans to buy Esso gasoline and "put a Tiger in your tank," advertising agencies began picking up on the tiger theme and applied it to push a multitude of products. Soon the striped beasts were everywhere. The word tiger had worked itself into the lexicon of the day, and every young man wanted to be a tiger, or at least wrap himself in that swinging image.

Pontiac had also used the tiger theme in several Tempest ads in 1963, but it didn't actually spread across the product line, nor did Pontiac aggressively image the Tempest that way. And while Pontiac didn't start out to promote the GTO as a tiger, it didn't take long for Wangers to recognize a good thing when he saw it, and the tiger concept slowly crept into some of the 1964 GTO advertising. "The GTO began to gather the image of the tiger," Wangers explained. "And quite honestly, this wasn't necessarily some-

This 1965 Teal Turquoise GTO is well known in the GTO hobby. Owned by Chuck Roberts since 1968, this GTO sports a set of Grand Prix parking lamps in the grille and Cragar SS wheels.

thing that we went out front to promote. It just kind of happened."

The tiger theme began to snowball thanks to US Royal, which supplied tires for many GM products, and had produced the redline tire for the 1964 GTO. The redlines contributed to the GTO's capability to endlessly burn rubber, not because the car had such a tremendous amount of torque but because the skinny 7.75x14 in. tires had such a small footprint on the ground. For 1965, these redlines were dubbed Tiger Paws and US Royal launched a massive TV and print advertising campaign. After all, the name Tiger Paw was far more appealing than Super–Safety 800, the model designation for the four-ply bias-belted tire.

The GTO was a benefactor of the US Royal campaign. "We really kind of fell into it," Wangers said. "It was a label that grew onto the car because the tires were original equipment and we were the only car to offer the Tiger Paw. It was a logical conclusion: what has a tiger paw on it but a tiger?"

Pontiac constructed a major advertising campaign capitalizing on the tiger theme, starting at the dealer level, with black-and-gold striped paper covering the showroom windows. Added to this

The GTO owner could also modify the underhood to suit his tastes. The use of chrome was very popular, and although Pontiac chromed the valve covers and air cleaner lid, there was plenty more virgin metal for the owner to chromeplate. The Ram Air tub (part of the over-the-counter cold-air accessory package) replaced the air cleaner bases and sealed to the underhood using a thick rubber gasket.

were tiger tails that hung from the fuel filler door in the bumper or emerging from the hood and draped across the fender. Television ads depicted a growling tiger leaping into the engine bay of a GTO. Pontiac magazine advertising proclaimed, "You don't know what a real tiger is until you hear this GeeTO Tiger growl!"

The Wide Track Pontiac Tiger campaign swept the nation, along with men's GTO cologne, GTO shoes and the "GeeTO Tiger," a three-minute song with the California surfer sound that was little more than a musical commercial for the GTO. On the flip side was a test drive of the GTO, in which the listener imagined himself riding shotgun while the announcer took a GTO through its paces on the test track. Imagination was precisely what it took, because in reality a stock GTO could hardly perform as the record indicated (the entire recording was done in a studio). Available from Pontiac for fifty cents, the record was also used to tie in a special promotion with Hurst. Advertisements by Hurst appeared in national car magazines like *Hot Rod* announcing a contest in which anyone who listened to the "GeeTO Tiger" recording, correctly counted the number of times the word tiger was used and explained "why I would like to own the original GeeTO Tiger," could send in their answer and be eligible to win the Grand Prize—a 1965 GTO with special Tiger Gold paint, gold-anodized Hurst wheels and a gold-plated Hurst shifter.

All of this promotion transformed the GTO's image far beyond its true street performance capabilities. Pontiac knew the hydraulic-lifter 389 couldn't outgun a Super Stock Plymouth or a Z–11 Chevrolet and avoided any type of comparison with these cars, which just two years before had been the only game in town. "We knew the only way we were going to survive was to take this car and equate

Peeking out from beneath the open scoop ornament is the chrome lid of a Tri-Power air cleaner. The optional cold-air package included a spare ornament that was opened by the owner and a tub that sealed to the underhood. The blast of cold air was said to be good for extra horsepower under hard acceleration.

The heart of the GTO was its engine, and the Tri-Power was Pontiac's high-performance jewel. It was docile at low speeds, possessed plenty of torque and didn't require a lot of maintenance. Rated at 360 hp, the Tri-Power could propel the GTO through the quarter in the low- to mid-fourteens straight off the showroom floor.

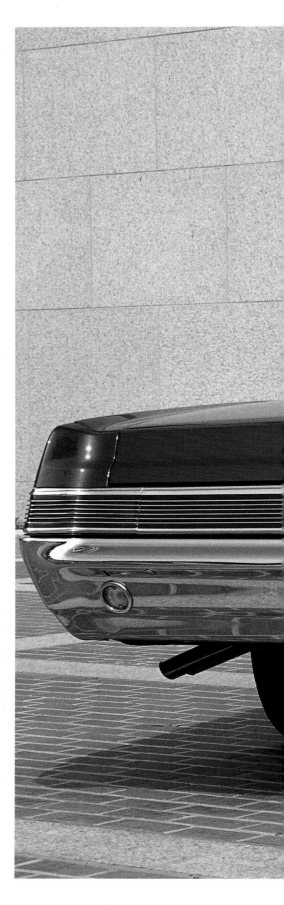

Previous page
The original GeeTO Tiger giveaway car still exists and is in good condition. The Hurst wheels and gold-plated shifter are still intact.

The Hurst shifter was standard equipment on every GTO built.

A popular showroom item was the tiger tail attached to the fuel filler door. The Tiger theme was used in the showrooms and in magazine and television advertising.

it more into a lifestyle," Wangers recalled. This was one of the reasons options like a dual four-barrel induction setup was scrapped, although the new single-scoop hood, which was actually planned for 1966, was placed on the 1965 GTO in anticipation of the canceled dual-quad option.

Pontiac gave the Tempest line a facelift in 1965, changing the headlamps from horizontal to vertical, much like the large Pontiacs had received beginning in 1963. The split-grille theme was retained and a large Pontiac crest was added between the deep-set grilles. For the GTO, the grilles were blacked out. The GTO nameplate seemed to float in the black left-hand grille, making it instantly recognizable from the more pedestrian Tempest and LeMans.

The flanks were virtually the same as on the 1964, as was the greenhouse. The rear was revised, featuring eight thin bars that ran across the back, stretching between the taillamp bezels. The GTO nameplate remained on the rear quarter, and the wedge-shaped 6.5 Litre emblem continued on the front fenders behind the wheel opening.

Inside, the seats were reupholstered, with the seat center inserts ornamented by diagonal bars and the Pontiac crest embossed in the center of the seatback. On the door panels, a smaller version of the fender emblem was attached near the window crank. The center console was nearly identical to the 1964, however, the instrument panel was completely redesigned. A larger pad hooded the top of the instrument panel, and a passenger grab bar was placed directly above the glovebox door. The gauge panel retained the four-pod design of previous years. The standard gauge arrangement included a fuel gauge and speedometer, with telltale lamps for temperature, amps and oil pressure. A clock was optional.

A host of new options were offered for the 1965 GTO, including a Rally cluster. This gauge cluster placed the fuel gauge and battery telltale lamp in the left pod. In the second pod from the left was the 120 mph speedometer, odometer and a semi-furled checkered flag to

It was possible to load up the GTO with virtually every interior luxury such as air conditioning, power windows and tilt steering wheel. Combined with performance options like Tri-Power and a four-speed transmission, it was possible to build a true Grand Touring automobile.

Another example of what made the GTO special from other performance cars was the instrument package layout. While other manufacturers used a large, horizontal sweep speedometer and tiny, tacked-on gauges, the GTO's Rally cluster was housed in four large pods that were easy to read and looked like they belonged in a European sports car.

You don't know what a real tiger is

Roaring up a growl by cutting in the quad on the 335-horse job or opening up the triples on the 360 isn't the only charge you get from owning a GTO. Try handling a wicked curve with one and you will never look at those so-called sports cars again.

Same goes for the interior. All that carpeting and bucket seats make those expensive foreign machines look positively drab. Then there's the chrome-plated air cleaner, chrome-plated rocker covers, pinstriping, an all-synchro 3-speed Hurst shifter, and a reputation as fierce as a Bengal tiger's.

until you hear this GeeTO Tiger growl.

If you want a taste of what it's like to own a GTO, or if you already own one and like to lullaby yourself to sleep in style, send 50¢ (60¢ in Canada) for the swingingest record you ever heard. On one side there's The Big Sounds of the GeeTO Tiger—your chance to ride shotgun with a top Pontiac test driver as he puts the GTO through its paces at the GM Proving Ground. And on the flip side, the hit that's sure to sweep the country: GeeTO Tiger! Man, that's tiger talk. Send your half dollar to: GeeTO Tiger, P.O. Box 456F, 196 Wide-Track Blvd., Pontiac, Michigan. *(No stamps please.)*

Wide-Track Pontiac Tiger—GTO

Previous page
Two young ladies and a 1965 GTO convertible were the stars in one particular Pontiac television spot, out for a Sunday drive in the country. The commercial ends as the GTO returns at dusk to the city and the announcer coos, "It's the swingingest!" The 1965 GTO in Montero Red.

reinforce the rally theme. In the third pod was an 8000 rpm tachometer with a 250 degree sweep. It was much larger and easier to read than the small, 90 degree tach offered in 1964. In the fourth, far right-hand pod was a water temperature and oil pressure gauge. All characters and graduations were white on black dials, and a wood applique decorated the face of the gauge panel.

Other new interior options for 1965 included an AM-FM radio and three-spoke Custom Sport steering wheel. For

the first time, a wheel option was offered for the GTO. The silver-textured 14x6 in. Rally wheel was constructed of stamped steel and featured six cooling slots and a chromed center cap.

Under the new hood was a revised version of the 389 ci engine, sporting a new intake-manifold design with revised runners and ports. The cylinder-head passages were also new, however, intake and exhaust valves were still measured at 1.92 and 1.66 in., respectively. Camshaft profile was unchanged from the 1964 engine. The standard engine still utilized a Carter AFB four-barrel topped by a redesigned chrome air cleaner with louvers in the cleaner's circumference, appearing quite similar to the Corvette. Horsepower for the base engine was upped to 335 at 5000 rpm, with 431 lb-ft of torque at 3200 rpm.

The optional Tri-Power engine also featured the new intake-manifold-runner design, and shared the cylinder

Pontiac quickly learned that they had a tiger by the tail with the GTO, and by the time of this ad in the May 1965 issue of Car and Driver *magazine, the GTO was now the GeeTO Tiger with tiger tail streaming from the hood. Tagged to the ad was the release of "GeeTO Tiger," a special record offered by Pontiac for fifty cents. The record cover pictured a tiger skin adorning the hood of a yellow GTO.*

heads and block, 10.75:1 pistons, Arma-Steel connecting rods and cast pearlitic malleable-iron crankshaft with the base engine. Tri-Power engines mated to the two-speed automatic transmission continued to use vacuum-controlled secondaries, but stick-shift models now featured mechanical linkages for the outer carburetors. The camshaft timing was a tad higher, at 288 degrees duration for intake and 302 degrees duration exhaust. In Tri-Power configuration, the

GTO was rated at 360 hp at 5200 rpm and delivered 424 lb-ft at 3600 rpm. Cast-iron exhaust manifolds dumped the spent gases through dual exhausts with reverse-flow mufflers and resonators.

Four transmissions were available in 1965, starting with a two-speed automatic with either standard column mount or optional console location. Three manual gearboxes were on the order sheet—a three-speed with floor-mounted shifter, and two four-speeds, one close-ratio with a 2.20:1 first gear, and a wide-ratio with a 2.56:1 first gear. All manual boxes were stirred by a Hurst shifter; a center console was optional with the stick shifts. Rear-axle ratios ranged from an economical 3.08:1 up to gut-wrenching 4.33:1 cogs that could be ordered with any transmission and required the extra-cost heavy-duty radiator, power brakes, metallic brake linings and limited-slip rear options.

The suspension was unchanged from 1964, with independent front suspension using unequal-length upper and lower control arms, coil springs, hydraulic shock absorbers and antisway bar. Around back, the four-link rear was used with a live axle, coil springs and hydraulic shock absorbers. Manual steering was slow, with a ratio of 24:1 and a hefty four turns lock to lock. Power assist was faster with a 17:1 ratio.

The weakest link in the GTO package—the brakes—was unchanged from 1964. The metallic linings were again offered; however, in an effort to improve the GTO's braking capabilities, an aluminum front drum option was now on the order sheet. The finned aluminum units were designed to dissipate heat more efficiently and improve braking.

At 3,700 lb., the GTO was no lightweight, but it was 500–600 lb. lighter than full-sized high-performance cars. In pure stock configuration, the 360 hp GTO could turn the quarter in 14.5 seconds at 100 mph. Dropping the exhausts, advancing the timing and bolting on a set of slicks dropped that to 14.06 at 102 mph. As the late Roger Huntington observed, "the quarter-mile times should win the B/Stock class on a good many dragstrips around the country on a given Sunday afternoon."

Because of the tremendous success enjoyed by Pontiac in 1965, with the GTO in particular and the entire product

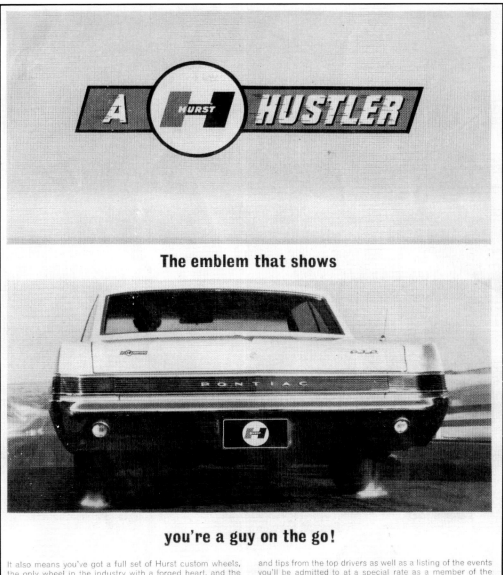

A HURST HUSTLER

The emblem that shows

you're a guy on the go!

It also means you've got a full set of Hurst custom wheels, the only wheel in the industry with a forged heart, and the safest, strongest wheel you can buy. The "Hurst Hustler Club" is a plus feature.

Get a set, or a pair if you're pressed, and send in the warranty cards. (This guarantees your Hurst wheels for as long as you own them.) Once you have *four*, we'll send you your membership card, a jacket patch and a set of three Hurst Hustler car emblems that single you out as a guy who's going places, a guy who won't settle for second best.

As a member you'll receive Hurst's new monthly publication that will present performance secrets

and tips from the top drivers as well as a listing of the events you'll be admitted to at a special rate as a member of the "Hustlers." Your membership card will also serve as a pass to get you into the "House of Hurst"—a hospitality lounge at major events that will offer surprises and special features strictly for members.

The new Hurst wheel *alone* is reason enough to join the "Hustlers." With all the rest that's offered—the prestige and advantages of belonging to the newest, most exclusive national performance organization . . . what're you waiting for! Get down to your local speed shop and get a set. For wheel details write Hurst Performance Products, Glenside, Pa.

line in general, the division won the *Motor Trend* Car of the Year award for the entire product line-up. It was one of the last public accolades Pete Estes would field as general manager of Pontiac Motor Division. In June of 1965, Estes was promoted to general manager of Chevrolet and John Z. DeLorean was

The Pontiac-Hurst relationship ran deep. It was unusual for Hurst not to use a Pontiac product in their mid-1960s advertising. To become a Hurst Hustler, all one needed to do was purchase a set of Hurst wheels and send in the membership form. Along with a jacket patch and a membership card came three Hurst Hustler emblems that the owner could proudly install on his car.

The Hurst wheel and the redline tire were a knockout in 1965.

US Royal, original equipment suppliers of the redline tire for the GTO, quickly launched their own ad campaign in the tail end of the 1964 model year, capitalizing on the tiger theme. The Tiger Paw campaign was recently resurrected by the company, now known as Uniroyal.

elevated to the top spot at Pontiac. The last member of the Knudsen-Estes-DeLorean triumvirate that would rule over Pontiac's successful reign as America's performance car builder was in the driver's seat. The number-three sales position firmly belonged to Pontiac, and with the brilliant young DeLorean at the helm, the future gleamed. DeLorean was attuned to the youth market and understood what it took to market cars like the GTO to the eighteen- to twenty-five-year-old market, which was coming into its own as a huge consumer base. Wangers continued to monitor the trends on the street and telegraph them to DeLorean. He recognized what image and profile accomplished, and that marketing was as important as styling and engineering.

"We put the GTO and its image in the drive-in and we put it in the record machine and we put it in the minds of

Hurst and the GTO

The relationship between George Hurst and Pontiac was firmly established in the early 1960s. Pontiac was the first to offer Hurst's stout three-speed floorshifter, and Estes and Wangers had urged Hurst to develop a four-speed shifter, which he did in 1961. Pontiac immediately put it in their order book. When the GTO arrived in 1964, it was equipped with the Hurst lever, and every manual gearbox GTO built until 1974 was stirred with a Hurst stick.

When Hurst decided to build aftermarket wheels, he constructed them with the same bulletproof engineering that went into his shifters. In the early 1960s, aftermarket wheels were prone to breakage because in the manufacturers' zeal for light weight or styling, lateral load capabilities were less than adequate, and many wheels failed, often causing accidents. George Hurst chose to build an unbreakable wheel.

Hurst built his wheel center out of forged aluminum alloy with heavy-duty steel rims. The rims featured a load-distributing stabilizer plate welded to the rim, and by riveting *and* welding the center section to the rim, the wheel was virtually

unbreakable. Dubbed The Dazzler by Hurst because of its zinc diachromate coloration, the Hurst wheel could be personalized by choosing one of twenty-four different combinations of beauty ring finish, rim bead design and center spoke finish. The Hurst wheel wasn't cheap, priced at $69.50 less lug nuts in the Hurst catalog, but then Hurst was selling safety, construction and styling. The wheels were assigned individual serial numbers for theft protection, and Hurst issued an unconditional guarantee against wheel failure because of faulty design or manufacture.

The Hurst wheel was introduced to the public, tied into the GTO. Because of the Name the Tiger contest conducted by Hurst, Pontiac and Petersen Publications, publishers of *Hot Rod* and *Motor Trend*, the GTO was chosen to pace the *Motor Trend* Riverside 500, and the wheel was introduced at a large press bash in Los Angeles on January 5, 1965, mounted on several GTOs, including one dressed out as the pace car for the race.

Although the wheel was superbly built (it was certified for race use by the NHRA), very handsome and highly advertised by Hurst, the wheel was one of Hurst's few marketing failures.

65

To many owners, the GTO is also an opportunity to express one's personal statement. Some GTO owners have taken their favorite components from various years and combined them. This particular 1965 interior sports a 1964 Custom Sport wheel and 1967 seats, door and quarter trim panels.

Previous page
Part of what made the GTO stand out from its rivals was the execution of the interior. The driver's seating position, the instrumentation and the overall ergonomics were second only to the Corvette.

The rear seat was roomy and comfortable, however, legroom was cramped for adults.

The 1965 GTO had a taut, aggressive stance. Heavy-duty springs and shocks were standard, as was a front antisway bar. The split-grille styling was a Pontiac trademark that had originated in 1959.

The words GTO 6.5 Litre also appeared on door panels for the first time in 1965.

young people," Wangers recollected with pride. "We began to equate the fact that a car was much like a suit of clothes or a pair of shoes. It was the kind of thing that you personified yourself with. And very quickly, almost overnight, there were young guys who were driving a GTO because the GTO had suddenly become accepted much the same as the Corvette had been. The GeeTO Tiger campaign and its success was really one of the most fun periods that any manufacturer went through."

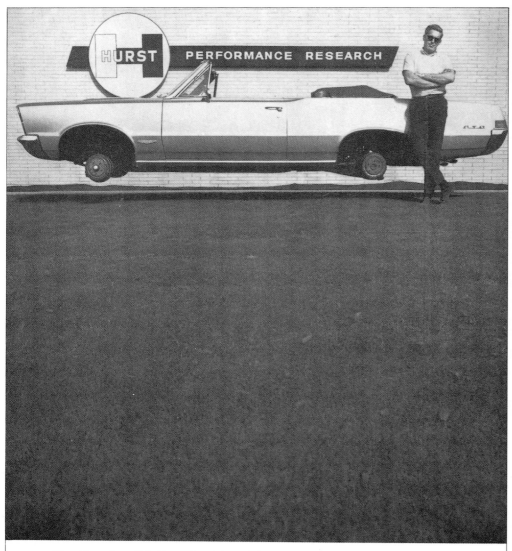

The product announcement for the new Hurst wheel was unusual in that it didn't show the product. All that's pictured is this 1965 GTO convertible floating in air, awaiting its new set of Hurst wheels.

The 1965 GTO in Burgundy. The bubble-styled hood scoop was first planned for 1966 but then moved up a year in anticipation of a dual four-barrel carburetor option. The option was canceled, but the hood was retained for 1965.

For 1965, a grab bar was installed above the glovebox next to the GTO nameplate.

Back in the mid-1960s, a Hurst-equipped emblem was a badge of honor to be worn by musclecars sporting Hurst equipment.

Count the tigers!

Listen to the Colpix recording "GeeTO Tiger" by the Tigers (a great new group of swingers!), and count the number of times the word *tiger* is sung in the record. (Complete rules are listed below.)

And win one in the HURST-GeeTO Tiger Contest!

Win the original GeeTO Tiger—a wild '65 GTO with special Hurst-gold paint and unique tiger-appointed interior. It's set up to *go*. Features Pontiac's big-gun 360-hp mill with 3 deuce carbs, transistorized ignition and 4-speed close ratio box with a gold-plated Hurst shifter. All riding on a full set of gold anodized Hurst custom wheels. Wild!

(To see a "live one" stop by your local Pontiac dealer's. He's got his own version of this one-of-a-kind Hurst hustler.)

6 more prizes from Hurst!

To runner-up winners Hurst is giving away: two sets of Hurst custom wheels. Two Competition Plus 4-speed shifters. And two Synchro/Loc 3-speed shifters.

JUNE 1965

100! Prizes! 100!

Still more. Like auto-stereos. Record albums from Colpix Recordings. And subscriptions to *Hot Rod, Motor Trend, Car Craft, Rod & Custom*, and *Teen*. The editors of these magazines are honorary judges and will assist George Hurst in selecting the winners. Their decision is final.

One more time!

All you have to do is: 1) Listen to the record "GeeTO Tiger" by the Tigers. 2) Put down on a sheet of paper the number of times the word *tiger* is sung in the record. 3) On the same sheet write, in 25 words or less, "Why I would like to own the original GeeTO Tiger"—the car that inspired the song. 4) Send

your entries to:
**Hurst Performance Products
P. O. Box X509, Dept. "HR"
Glenside, Pa.**

That's all you have to do. But do it quick. Entries must be postmarked no later than July 31, 1965 and become the property of Hurst Performance Products. Contest not valid where prohibited by state or local law.

43

Tied in to the other GTO ads hyping the GTO Tiger and the record was this promotion, put together by Petersen Publishing Company, Hurst and Pontiac. Grand prize was a loaded GTO, equipped with Hurst wheels and a gold-plated shifter. To enter, all one needed to do was count the number of words in the song "GeeTO Tiger" and include a reason for wanting to own the original GeeTO Tiger.

The 1965 GTO received minor styling changes. The quad headlamps were revised from horizontal to vertical, and the grilles were deep set and blacked out. The GTO emblem appeared in the left-hand grille.

The GTO nameplate adorned the quarter panels and the deck lid. A single pinstripe ran the length of the upper beltline from head-lamp to taillamp.

Next page
Riding on a 115 in. wheelbase, the 1965 GTO was a nimble-handling, quick-accelerating package that was hard to beat on the street or strip.

The relationship between Car and Driver *and the GTO continued beyond the infamous 1964 road test that elevated the GTO to Ferrari status, in the eyes of* Car and Driver. *This ad was Pontiac's rebuttal to the many letters the magazine received taking them to task for their editorial blasphemy against the Italian sports car.*

Ram Air, Royal Pontiac and the GTO

The idea of tamping cold air into a high-performance engine had already been well proven on the drag strip; Pontiac racers had installed scoops on the hoods of their 1962 Super Duty Catalinas. When the GTO was introduced, testing was already under way on developing a cold-air package for the street. Because of the design of the 1964 GTO's hood-scoop ornaments, which flanked each side of the hood line and were more scalloped than scooped, a cowl-induction setup, similar to that used in NASCAR, was tested and abandoned.

With the proposed dual-quad setup for the 1965 GTO, a new scoop design was devised, placing the bubble at the hood centerline and capping the opening with a pot-metal ornament retained by three speednuts. This hood would be standard on all GTOs. Dual-quad cars would be available with a cold-air package, consisting of a metal tub or "pan" installed on the carburetors, taking the place of the air-cleaner base. The outer edges of the tub would curl upward and be lined with a thick rubber gasket that, when the hood was closed, would seal out the hot underhood air. The solid ornament would be replaced by an open unit that allowed outside air to be "rammed" into the carburetors under wide-open throttle to increase horsepower.

When the dual-quad option was canceled, a decision was made to leave the hood on the car with the closed ornament installed. It was, however, not the end of the cold-air package. Thanks to testing conducted by Royal Pontiac and Pontiac Engineering, a new air-scoop accessory package was released on August 17, 1965. Available to dealers to sell over the counter, the $49.50 package (part number 984716) was designed to fit the Tri-Power induction setup and consisted of the tub, gasket, a closed scoop ornament and instructions on removing the rear section of the forward hood bracing and opening the replacement ornament. The design and construction of the components was similar to the ill-fated dual-quad cold-air package.

While it would be several more years before becoming available as a production option and officially designated Ram Air, the 1965 air scoop package was the first cold-air induction system for the GTO.

Standard equipment on all 1965 GTOs was the 7.75x14 in. US Royal bias-belt redline tire. If the optional Deluxe, Custom or wire wheel cover or the Rally wheel was not ordered, the basic hubcap was installed. Many buyers pitched the factory wheel covers for a set of Cragars or chrome reversed wheels.

The Custom Spinner wheel disc was an extra-cost item and featured six cooling slots and the words Pontiac Motor Division in the center of the three-eared spinner.

1966 GTO

The Juggernaut Rolls On

When the 1966 GTO was introduced in September 1965, DeLorean's stewardship as Pontiac general manager was only a few months old. The 1966 model year would prove to be pivotal in the history of the GTO for several reasons. Most significantly, the GTO matured from an option package based on the LeMans to a separate series with its own 242 model designation. Thanks to the resounding success Pontiac had enjoyed with the GTO in 1964 and 1965, the future of the GTO was ensured for at least the next five model years. Sales of the 1964 GTO had tallied 32,450 units and the 1965 GTO had surpassed Pontiac's projection of 50,000 units by a total of 75,352 cars. With the tremendous success of the GTO in the showroom, Pontiac penciled in sales projections in the 80,000 range for 1966.

Another factor in the GTO's elevation to series status was the climate within General Motors. GM management had

Around back, the GTO had a set of louvered taillamps, trimmed by bright eyebrows and the name Pontiac spelled out in large block letters. The chrome exhaust tips were optional.

come around to the concept of the musclecar, and the engine displacement ceiling for mid-sized cars was raised to 400 ci. Buick, Oldsmobile and Chevrolet were given the corporate nod to aggressively field their own versions of the GTO. Oldsmobile's 4-4-2, which had been released in the tail end of the 1964 model year, had grown into a 400 ci contender in 1965, and for 1966 offered a three two-barrel induction system, its first since the J-2 option of the late 1950s. Buick's Gran Sport was repackaged with the 401 and upgraded options; however, at 340 hp, small exhaust valves and no specific performance camshaft, it still was no match for the GTO. Sister division Chevrolet was the biggest in-house threat to the GTO. The SS396 Chevelle was offered in three horsepower versions—the base 325 hp, 360 hp and a thumping 375 hp engine that was available on special order.

Ford and Chrysler weren't sitting on their hands while the GTO and other GM musclecar programs were gathering strength. Ford's weakness was their lack of a large-displacement engine to drop into the redesigned 1966 Fairlane and Mercury Comet. The GT and GTA were added to the Fairlane line-up, equipped

GTO stands for *Gran Turismo Omologato*. You've probably heard of it. A Pontiac in a saber-toothed tiger skin. The deceptively beautiful body comes in convertible, sports coupe, and hardtop configurations. With pinstriping. On a heavy-duty suspension system that thinks it's married to the ground. Bucket seats and carpeting. Wood-grained dash. Redlines or whitewalls at no extra cost. Chromed 335-hp 4 barrel under the hood. Fully-synchronized 3-speed on the column. Or order a heavy-duty all-synchro 3-speed or 4-speed with Hurst floor shifter. Or 2-speed auto. Or the 360-hp 3 2-BBL. There's a catalog full of options. See if you can get your Pontiac dealer to cough one up. That's the GTO/2+2 performance catalog. You'll recognize it. It vibrates.

Speak softly and carry a GTO

On the high banks at the GM proving grounds, this 1966 GTO barreling by was one of the last speed-oriented ads to be run by Pontiac. New corporate guidelines issued by GM for 1967 forbade these types of ads from appearing in the future.

with the venerable 390 ci FE engine that produced 335 hp. Mercury's Cyclone GT was a carbon copy of the Fairlane GT. At the tail end of the model year, a few of these cars received the 425 hp, 427 ci engine, but it was produced in limited numbers, mostly to enhance the product line's image. Combined sales of the Fairlane GT and Cyclone GT were a disappointment to Ford, barely breaking the 53,000 unit mark.

Chrysler was in a much stronger position to counter the success of the GTO, and they rolled out the heavy artillery in 1966 in the form of the street Hemi. Dodge also released the new fastback Charger in January of 1966. Although the majority of Chargers were sold with the more mundane 318 and 361 two-barrel engines, both Dodge and Plymouth offered the 325 hp 383 ci engine and the pavement-melting 426 Hemi. Interestingly enough, the Hemi-powered Plymouth Satellite, with 425 hp—65 more than the Tri-Power GTO—only turned the quarter a few tenths quicker than a Royal-prepared GTO, although *Popular Hot Rodding* did record 13.25 seconds at 109.9 mph in a 1966 Hemi Satellite.

All this competition did little to slow the GTO's momentum. At the end of the model year, Pontiac's cash register rang to the tune of 96,946 units as the GTO sales juggernaut rolled on. The Wide Track Tiger was simply too entrenched in the minds of young, performance-minded enthusiasts, and Wangers' genius in promoting the GTO's image was a major contributing factor in the GTO holding back the wave of fledgling competitors.

Much of the GTO's appeal in 1966 can be attributed to Pontiac's handsome restyling effort. Although still riding the same 115 in. wheelbase, all the GM intermediates were reskinned for 1966, and the GTO seemed to benefit the most from the restyling. In fact, it looked more like the full-sized Grand Prix, and it attracted buyers who were drawn to the Grand Prix's styling but resisted the high sticker price and the dimensions of the larger model.

Pontiac again expanded the GTO's option list in 1966, and upgraded the car's interior appointments. According to Wangers: "A maturer performance market emerged as a significant factor, and we felt that perhaps some people might be turned off by the Grand Prix or the Bonneville as being just too big. We thought they may be looking for some kind of personal sophistication in a little smaller package."

When the sales figures for the 1965 and 1966 Grand Prix are examined, a case can be made that the GTO possibly did purloin some potential customers from the GP. Sales of the 1965 Grand Prix totaled 56,881, while 1966 GP sales turned down to 36,757 (excluding chassis sales, which totaled 643 in 1965 and 553 in 1966). Whether the GTO is directly responsible for the decline in 1966 GP

Options like the three-spoke Custom Sport steering wheel and tilt steering column were again available. The instrument panel fascia was covered in real wood veneer.

The diecast GTO emblem was located on the front fenders. A smaller version of the emblem appeared on the door panels.

sales is conjectural; however, it is interesting to note that GTO sales went up 21,594 units in 1966 while Grand Prix sales went down 21,124 units. How significant the GTO was to the decline in GP sales will never be fully ascertained.

The restyling of the 1966 GTO started at the front. The thematic Pontiac split-grille style was retained, but the grilles were plastic like the GP and deep set, with the parking-turn signal lamps

Standard in the GTO was this 389 ci engine, rated at 335 hp. Under the chrome-louvered air cleaner was a Carter AFB four-barrel carburetor.

incorporated into the grille, also like the GP. The Pontiac crest was moved to the hood, and the air scoop bubble and ornament were identical to 1965. Although the flanks were devoid of chrome trim, a bright rocker panel molding extended from the rear of the front-wheel opening to the front of the rear-wheel opening. Brightwork also trimmed the wheel openings. A single, thin pinstripe traced the upper beltline. The 6.5 Litre emblem was retained on the trailing edge of the lower front fenders and the GTO nameplate was affixed to the quarter panels. A smaller GTO nameplate was attached to the deck lid. The taillamp panel was cleaned up, with the name Pontiac spelled out in block letters and thin, bright eyebrows trimming the taillamp louvers again, similar to the Grand Prix.

The rooftop was redesigned, with curved side glass and the sail panels extended back in a semi-fastback effect; the rear glass was more vertically inset into the C-pillars. As in previous years, a hardtop and sport coupe were offered in 1966, along with a convertible.

The standard wheels were stamped steel and adorned by a simple hubcap with the words Pontiac Motor Division spelled out. Deluxe, Custom and wire wheel covers were offered optionally, as was the 14x6 in. Rally wheel. The Rally wheel was similar to the 1965 version, but the center cap was now painted black. As expected, US Royal 7.75x14 in.

Three Options That Never Were

There were three options considered for the 1966 model year that were never released.

Pontiac's beautiful aluminum eight-lug wheel with integral hub and drum had been an extremely popular option on the big cars, and development work had been ongoing for a version of the eight-lug for the intermediate models. This wheel was constructed of cast iron, utilized the same hub and drum assembly and was retained by eight chrome-plated socket-head Allen bolts threaded into the brake drum. It was to be offered on all Tempest, LeMans and GTO models in an attempt to improve the series' woeful braking system. By using twenty-four radial cooling fins, the gain in heat dissipation over the separate iron drum would provide better braking characteristics and longer brake-lining life. It was canceled just prior to production because the wheel was too heavy and too costly to produce.

DeLorean was impressed by the sophistication of European sport sedans, and wanted to meld some of the engineering philosophy from the Continent into Pontiac's design. In 1966–1967, the overhead-cam six-cylinder Tempest-LeMans Sprint was as close as an American car maker came to what BMW and Mercedes were building. DeLorean had also toyed with a radial tire option in 1966, even to the point of naming Michelin as an OE (original equipment) supplier. American tire manufacturers had not yet perfected their version of the radial tire, which was popular in Europe. DeLorean recognized the radial tire's superior ride and handling characteristics, and wanted them for the GTO. Pressure from American OE tire companies forced the cancellation of the option before 1966 production began.

Another option DeLorean had favored for several years was The Tiger Button. An under-the-dash handle would open baffles in the mufflers, reducing back pressure and thus improving performance and increasing the exhaust note. The Tiger Button was kicked around for several years before it was finally released as the Vacuum Operated Exhaust in the beginning of the 1970 model year. The option was short-lived; Pontiac canceled it less than two months after the 1970 models had been released.

The cold-air package was again offered as an over-the-counter package. However, in February 1966, Pontiac released the 360 hp XS option, which included a higher-lift camshaft, stiffer valve springs with dampers and the air cleaner tub and extra scoop ornament packed in the trunk for dealer installation.

A thin chrome bar outlined the trailing edge of the deck lid and the quarter panels. A single pinstripe ran along the upper beltline from the end of the quarter panel to the headlamp bezel.

redline Tiger Paw tires were standard. Whitewalls were available on request.

Inside, the GTO's interior was completely restyled. The dash pad was larger and extended from door to door, with a deep overhang above the instrument panel. The grab bar over the glovebox was redone, and the instrument panel fascia was enlarged and covered by a real wood applique.

The four-pod gauge layout was retained from previous years, and stan-

The GTO was completely restyled for 1966. The Coke-bottle flair of the rear quarter panels, begun with the 1963 Grand Prix, is very prominent in this profile view of a Montero Red convertible.

M&H Race Master slicks were popular at the drags in the mid-sixties. This Royal-prepared 1966 with Tri-Power could still light 'em up off the line, even with sticky M&H rubber.

The wire wheel disc option featured a two-eared spinner and looked like a real wire wheel.

Royal Pontiac continued to build and sell their Bobcat-equipped GTOs in 1966. The Bobcat decal, which appeared on the C-pillars on 1964–1965, was now affixed to the front fenders, just behind the bumper wrap-around.

A new option for all A-body Pontiac models was red plastic fender liners. The fender liners were constructed from heavy-gauge plastic and molded to fit inside the front and rear wheelhouses and were retained by screws. They improved the looks of the GTO and kept salt and dirt out of the wheelhouse. The Rally wheel was mostly unchanged from 1966. The center cap, chromed in 1965, was now painted matte black.

The vertical headlamp theme was continued from 1965. The grilles, however, were revised and were constructed of plastic, a first for Pontiac. The plastic grilles also appeared on the 1966 Grand Prix.

The driving lights for the GTO were mounted within the grilles.

dard instrumentation was a combination of telltale lamps, a fuel gauge and speedometer. An optional Rally clock, placed in the far right-hand pod, was available only with the standard gauge cluster. The Rally gauge cluster was carried over from 1965. The left-hand pod contained the fuel gauge and the battery telltale lamp. The left center pod housed the 120 mph speedometer and an odometer. An 8000 rpm tachometer with 5200 rpm redline was in the right-center pod, and the water temperature and oil pressure gauges resided in the far right-hand pod. The alphanumeric characters on the gauges were white on a green field. Accessory switches, such as power top, rear speaker fader or power antenna, were located above the gauge cluster, attached to the lower side of the instrument panel ledge. Controls and switches for wipers, headlamps, ignition and cigar lighter were below the gauges on the cluster fascia. The standard steering wheel was a solid, two-spoke design, and could be upgraded by the three-spoke Custom Sport wheel option, which was unchanged from the 1965 model.

The bucket seats were redesigned, with more padding and featuring horizontally rib-patterned upholstery. Two new seat options included a reclining

Starring with the Monkees in the hit TV show was a specially designed 1966 GTO, created by California customizer Dean Jeffries.

The Monkeemobile

Consistent with Jim Wangers' aggressive marketing efforts, the GTO appeared on a number of television shows in 1966. Pontiac sponsored the popular "My Three Sons," and a variety of Pontiac products were always prominent in many scenes. The character Maj. Tony Nelson in the "I Dream Of Jeannie" TV show also drove a GTO convertible.

Perhaps one of the most famous cars on TV in 1966 was the Monkeemobile, which transported the rock group The Monkees both on their TV show and at live appearances around the country. The brainchild of Wangers, the Monkeemobile was the creation of Los Angeles car customizer Dean Jeffries. Pontiac supplied Jeffries with a 1966 GTO convertible as a base. The car was equipped with the standard 335 hp engine and automatic transmission. Jeffries cut away the floor and trunk pan and altered the rear suspension, installing semi-elliptical springs and reinstalling a new floor. He retained the basic taillamp design; however, a center compartment was fabricated to house a drag chute.

The front and rear sheet metal were lengthened, and a new nose was designed utilizing the stock grilles. A nonfunctional GMC 671 blower was bolted onto the 389 and a custom interior with four-bucket seats was installed, with another seat in the open trunk. Since Pontiac had picked up the bill for Jeffries' work, they viewed it appropriate that the GTO emblems appear on the fenders and the GTO nameplate remain in the front grille. The show's producers, however, felt it would be difficult to attract other car makers to purchase commercial time, so the GTO nameplate on the grille was removed.

Two Monkeemobiles were eventually built. One went on tour with the band and, according to Jeffries, was left in Australia. The other was used for the television show and is today in the hands of a private collector. It occasionally is displayed at major automotive events.

Extensions were added to the front and rear fenders. Dean Jeffries trial-fits the stock left-hand GTO grille to the new front end taking shape. The stock grilles were used along with the drivetrain and instrument panel.

The Monkeemobile started life as a 1966 GTO convertible equipped with the standard 335 hp engine and automatic transmission. The trunk and floor pans were modified, and the rear suspension was changed from four-link coil to semi-elliptical springs.

passenger seat and headrests, in keeping with the more luxurious upgrade of the overall interior. The door and quarter trim panels echoed the rib pattern of the seats, and the GTO emblem was mounted in the center of the door panels. A host of power and luxury accessories was offered in 1966, including AM-FM radio, tilt steering column, power driver's seat and power windows. The GTO office was considerably more posh in 1966.

While the GTO's exterior and interior were totally redesigned for 1966, the drivetrain and underpinnings were virtually a carbon copy of 1965; the only changes being a new cylinder head with the same valve diameters as 1965, and an enlargement of the center carburetor on Tri-Power engines.

An even-odd pattern of alternating styling and engineering cycles had begun in 1965 and would continue through 1971. In odd-numbered years, the drivetrains would be revised while in even-numbered years, major styling changes would take place. Consequently, the 1965 GTO received new drivetrains, while the body was only given a facelift. In 1966, the body was restyled, while the drivetrain was carried over. This cycle would hold true in 1967 (new engine and transmission, cosmetic styling changes); 1968 (major restyling, drivetrain retained); 1969 (new engine options, styling facelift); 1970 (same engines, new body style); and 1971 (new engines, cosmetic facelift).

One addition to the GTO engine line-up was quietly released in February of 1966. Designated XS (denoting the engine code), this was a factory-built Tri-Power Ram Air package. The over-the-counter, cold-air package that had been released in 1965 was again offered in 1966; however, the XS option went beyond just a carburetor air cleaner tub and open scoop element. The XS option also included a new camshaft (part number 9785744) and stiffer valve springs that used a single spring with an inner spiral flat metal damper instead of the usual inner and outer valve spring arrangement. The 744 camshaft had the same .406 in. lift as the Tri-Power camshaft, but the lobe profiles were different, with intake duration of 301 degrees and exhaust duration of 313 degrees, and an overlap of 76 degrees. The 744 cam would become part of the factory-installed Ram Air package offered from

At the drags in the mid-sixties, GTOs ran in B/Stock. All it took for a 360 hp Tri-Power Goat to turn mid- to high-twelves was some minor engine work, open headers and a set of slicks.

One of the first Pro-Stock drag cars was Clint Logan's Legend, *based out of Colorado. Logan's GTO was all-Pontiac, and that included Poncho power under the hood.*

Not all GTOs came with bucket seats and four speeds, as evidenced by this GTO convertible equipped with bench seat and automatic transmission on the column.

Previous page
The GTO interior was also redesigned for 1966. The instrument panel fascia was enlarged, but the traditional four-pod cluster was retained. Standard transmission was a three-speed manual with the shifter on the steering column. Few GTOs were so equipped. Most came with the Hurst floorshifter and four-speed gearbox.

1967 to the middle of the 1969 model year.

A set of mandatory options was required with the XS option. The buyer had to accept the M21 close-ratio, four-speed transmission, 4.33:1 rear gearing, limited-slip rear, heavy-duty fan and metallic brake linings. The XS engine was capable of propelling the two-ton 1966 GTO through the quarter mile in 13.91 seconds at more than 100 mph, about 0.2 second and 3 mph quicker than the standard Tri-Power.

The release of the XS option received little fanfare and, according to Pontiac historian Pete McCarthy, only 190 XS engines were built; it's estimated that approximately 185 GTOs received the XS option. Pontiac Engineering also experimented with a four-barrel version of the cold-air induction package for the 1966 GTO, using a smaller pan fitted over the Carter AFB carburetor. Although it was abandoned before the 1966 model year began, it, and the XS option, pointed the way for future GTO Ram Air engines.

The GTO had come a long way in just three years, selling more than 200,000 units and dominating its market niche. Next to the Ford Mustang, the Pontiac GTO had been the most successful new

The GTO nameplate was on the quarter panels and deck lid. The nameplate consisted of chrome letters faced with black on a chrome bar. The deck-lid nameplate was smaller than the ones that appeared on the quarters.

car ever launched by an American car maker. But internal and external forces beyond the control of John DeLorean or Jim Wangers were about to converge and have a profound effect on how the GTO was equipped, imaged and marketed. The GTO had reached its zenith as the dominant marque in the musclecar field, and the phenomenal success of 1966 would never again be duplicated.

The 1966 GTO, here in Fontaine Blue with Black vinyl top, was an excellent road car. The suspension was firm but not harsh.

Thanks to the new Strato bucket seats, tilt column and six-way power seat, any driver could find a comfortable seating position.

The bubble-style scoop was placed in the centerline of the hood and was nonfunctional on standard and Tri-Power GTOs. The ornament could be opened in conjunction with the over-the-counter cold-air package.

Buying a 1966 GTO

It's safe to say the GTO attracted a diverse range of buyers in 1966; not all GTO buyers were drag racers or street-performance enthusiasts. The market was expanded to include people who might want to buy a GTO for the element of performance or image, and who also wanted a personal car with a little more sophistication and a touch of luxury.

It was DeLorean's goal to image Pontiac as the BMW of America. Sagacious use of the order book could produce a luxurious, high-performance American sport sedan that rivaled the best European Grand Touring cars. After all, isn't that what GTO stood for?

Code	Description	Price
24217	GTO Hardtop Coupe	$2,847.00
062	Protection Group	50.66
071	Mirror Group	13.21
SPS	Paint—Special Color—Tiger Gold	83.20
802	Engine—389 3/2 BBL	113.33
782	Transmission—Automatic	194.84
CC	Tires—Redline 7.75x14 premium	NC
582	Air Conditioner—Custom	343.20
651	Brake Drums—H.D. Aluminum Front	49.08
472	Console	47.13
SVT	Cordova Top—White Code 291	84.26
422	Deck Lid Release—Remote Control	12.64
731	Differential—Safe-T-Track	36.86
448	Instrument Panel—Rally Gauge Cluster	84.26
522	Liners—Fender—Red	26.33
502	Power Brakes—Wonder Touch	41.60
564	Power Bucket Seat—L.H.	69.51
501	Power Steering—Wonder Touch	94.79
551	Power Windows	100.05
345	Radio—Push Button AM/FM & Electric Antenna	162.88
352	Rear Speaker—Verba-Phonic	52.66
621	Ride and Handling Package	3.74
574	Seats—Reclining with RH & LH Head Rests	84.26
471	Steering Wheel—Custom Sports	38.44
504	Tilt Steering Column	42.13
671	Transistor Ignition	73.67
452	Wheel Discs—Wire	69.51
Total Price		$4,819.24

1967 GTO

The Great One

By the middle of the 1966 model year, James Roche, the chairman of General Motors, had already been doing a slow burn about Pontiac's GeeTO Tiger and Wide Track Tigers advertising campaign. He simply didn't like it, and every magazine ad he read and every TV spot he watched just added to his anger.

Unaware of Roche's displeasure with the Tiger, the people at Pontiac were delighted with the success of the campaign. "We had taken the Tiger theme, which came right out of the GTO, and spread it over the whole line," Wangers recounted. "All of the Pontiacs were promoted around the Tiger image. That was when we really reached our maturity in terms of recognizing the value of the GTO as an entire image builder for the division."

Unfortunately, that argument failed to cut any wood with Roche: he ordered the Tiger be returned to its cage. Pontiac needed to find a new theme for 1967.

While Wangers and Pontiac's advertising agency worked to develop a new

The 1967 GTO in Regimental Red with White vinyl top. Exterior styling was little changed from 1966.

campaign for the GTO, Pontiac engineering was also faced with challenges from the fourteenth floor of the GM building. Bowing to insurance and auto safety groups, GM president Ed Cole passed the word that all multiple-carburetion options were to be discontinued before the end of the 1966 model year. The only exception was Corvette, which was slated for a tri-carb option on the 427 engine in 1967. Most affected would be Pontiac and its Tri-Power performance option.

The Pontiac Tri-Power had symbolized the division's top-of-the-line performance option since it had been introduced in 1957. Although the dual-quad Super Duty may have displaced the Tri-Power in terms of sheer thunder, on the street where reputations were made, the Tri-Power was king. Losing it now could have been considered a fatal blow to the GTO's image. But DeLorean and Bill Collins already had a more than suitable successor ready. They believed with the right hardware, GTO enthusiasts would soon forget multiple carburetion. Wangers remembered the obstacles placed in Pontiac's way in the spring of 1966: "It made things more difficult. It didn't hurt, we didn't put our heads in the sand

This pre-production 1967 GTO shows some interesting variations. The Rally wheels have nonstock center caps and the wheels are color-keyed to the body. The rear quarter nameplate is a decal, which wouldn't be used until 1968.

When Is a Goat Not a Goat?

With The Great One theme on the screen and in print, the GTO for 1967 took on a new air of sophistication. Pontiac positioned the GTO to still appeal to the street enthusiasts, but older buyers, professionals and women were targeted as potential customers. One theme Wangers was never able to sell to GM management was the name that still endears itself to the GTO—The Goat. Wangers put together an ad showing a young man standing in his driveway, a pail under his arm, posing with his freshly washed bright red GTO. The ad was titled, "A Boy and His Goat," and by submitting it to the corporation for approval, Wangers, who always had one ear to the pavement, was to discover just how out of touch GM management was with the language and the culture of high-performance enthusiasts.

"At that time, they (GM) had already initiated a corporate committee for all of the divisions to submit their advertising and get approval on everything before we could run it," Wangers recalled. "They were sort of policing the division to make sure we didn't break any of their policies."

Wangers felt the "Boy and His Goat" ad met the criteria. "The ad suggested that everyone ought to have a GTO in order to complete their life cycle," Wangers said. "The ad was very much in line with the pride of ownership image. We felt we had

been very successful in capturing that and thought this was an ad that set itself completely within the framework of what the corporation wanted and did for us what we wanted."

The corporate committee rejected the ad based on its perception of what the word goat defined. "The guys downtown told us a goat is the butt of a joke or the butt end of a mistake," Wangers commented. "And they said they certainly understood it enough to know they wouldn't approve it."

Wangers put together a study that quoted enthusiasts in the field, and assembled magazine articles that referenced the GTO as The Goat, and presented it to the committee, explaining, "You've got to give us the benefit of the doubt here, that we know what we're doing. The word Goat is an accepted nickname of the GTO in the field. The people who are living with this car and love and respect it have assumed that the word GTO stands for Goat. Allow us the professionalism of knowing our market. That's why we're successful."

The committee refused the appeal, responding that GM was not going to allow Pontiac to demean the name of their car by referring to it as a goat. Pontiac no longer had the freedom to image and market its products without corporate approval of all advertising. It was the end of a grand era of Tigers, and Wide Tracking would never be the same again.

The GTO emblem was moved from the fender to the rocker trim panel, which was higher and bolder than 1966.

and die and cry. We just rolled up our sleeves a little further and dug in a little deeper.''

Wangers' first responsibility was to set the tone for the 1967 GTO introduction. For the public to forget the Tiger, he needed a theme that would set a new direction for the GTO. "We took liberty with the initials GTO and came up with TGO—The Great One.'' Drawing on the GTO's image with the "kids on the street" and the reputation the GTO had earned as the premier musclecar, The Great One campaign was built around the 1967 model.

With the theme intact, there was one more hurdle to jump, this one also imposed by the corporation. The Federal Trade Commission, under increasing pressure from insurance lobbies and safety groups spearheaded by Ralph Nader, had advised car makers that high-performance models should not be advertised in ways that "promote racing or aggressive street driving.'' Always sensitive to government intervention, GM management distributed guidelines advising how the divisions could advertise their high-performance models. GM didn't want to see cars with dust flying, wheels spinning, leaning into curves or exiting curves at high speed. Ideally, the cars were to be presented in static reposes. They could be shown in motion; however, the motion used was

not to suggest or promote "aggressive driving.''

Wangers and the D'Arcy advertising staff developed a series of magazine ads depicting the 1967 GTO in a neutral studio environment, either touting its good looks, plethora of options or engine line-up. For television spots, actor Paul Richards was hired as Pontiac spokesman. Richards was cool and sophisticated—like John DeLorean—and smoothly delivered the new message about The Great One. As he walked around a GTO convertible in a darkened arena, the camera caressed the quarter panel's profile, then snapped to the grille emblem, wheel, hood and the interior. All the while Richards was making the message clear that the GTO was the Ultimate Driving Machine: "if you don't know

97

The 360 hp Ram Air engine. The Ram Air took over where the HO left off and added a more radical camshaft and stiffer valve springs. The only rear axle ratio offered was 4.33:1.

Previous page
The optional 360 hp HO 400 ci engine featured an open-element air cleaner, free-flowing cast-iron exhaust headers and high-lift camshaft.

what that means, then you're excused," Richards explained. "But if, when you see this car, you're seized with an uncontrollable urge to plant yourself behind the wheel and head for the wide-open spaces, then we're talking to you."

The Wide Track theme was still the foundation for Pontiac's main image, and for 1967, buyers were urged to "Ride the Wide Track Winning Streak." One TV commercial depicted two young ladies out for a cruise in a 1967 GTO convertible. The same composition had also been used in 1965 and 1966, and through the use of upbeat music, the idea was presented that driving a GTO was for pretty, sophisticated people. The message was simple: you could become sophisticated and attract females if you, too, drove a GTO.

While the battles for image and themes were going on, the solu-

tion to the end of the Tri-Power was much easier to find. Bill Collins and Pontiac Engineering had been ready for the Tri-Power's demise, and were ready to discard the Carter AFB as well in favor of a new series of Rochester Quadra-Jets. The new Q-Jets flowed more air than the old AFBs, and with a venturi area of 9.4 sq-in, the new Q-Jet would soon have Pontiac fans forgetting about the legendary Tri-Power.

For 1967, there were four engine choices, all now displacing 400 ci. This was the first time the 389 had been punched out since 1959. To achieve the new displacement, bore diameter was drilled out from 0.406 to 0.412 in.; the stroke remained constant at 3.75 in. The cylinder head was redesigned for improved volumetric flow. Part of its efficiency was achieved by moving the chamber to the center of the bore, thus permitting larger 2.11 in. intake and 1.77 in. exhaust valve diameters. The intake-port design flowed significantly better than previous heads, and also boasted screw-in rocker-arm studs and stamped-steel valve guides. The dual-plane intake manifold was redesigned to accept the Quadra-Jet and was plumbed for future emissions equipment, as was the 1967 head, which featured exhaust-port air-injection holes. Interestingly enough, port dimensions were identical to 1966, and quite a number of Pontiac enthusiasts took to bolting the 1966 Tri-Power

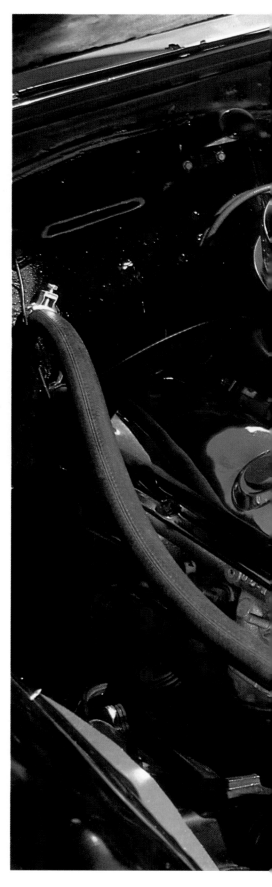

onto the 1967 engine. Some legends just die hard, it seemed.

The base 400 was rated at 335 hp at 5000 rpm. This engine was quite similar to the standard 1966 GTO engine, and utilized the same air cleaner, camshaft profile, valve springs and exhaust manifolds.

Optional at no cost was a low-compression, small-valve 255 hp 400 that was offered only with automatic transmission. It was the first time a nonperformance engine was installed in the GTO. Its introduction into the line-up was the result of the Marketing Department insisting on a low-compression engine available for the buyer who wanted the GTO image but not the horsepower or the GTO's unquenchable thirst for gas.

Next step up the engine option ladder was the new 360 hp 400 HO. The HO featured an open-element air cleaner, a slightly bumpier camshaft and cast-iron exhaust manifolds that were similar to the classic "long branch" headers from the 1962 Super Duty. These new headers separated the exhaust pulses beyond the

The changing of the guard took place in 1967, as Pontiac discontinued the legendary Tri-Power. After ten years as the division's top-performance engine option, the potent trio of Rochester two-barrel carburetors gave way to the new Rochester Quadra-Jet carburetor. Both are shown with their Ram Air tubs in the Pontiac Engineering garage.

The base engine was rated at 335 hp and displaced 400 ci.

ports and allowed the engine to exhale with less restriction.

At the top rung of the ladder was the Ram Air engine, also rated at a tongue-in-cheek 360 hp. All the usual Ram Air goodies were there like the open scoop ornament and the foam-lined tub around the carburetor, but now the four-barrel Q-Jet breathed through the HO's open element and exhaled freely thanks to the HO's exhaust headers. Inside, the Ram Air was a carbon copy of the 1966 XS

The Rally clock was optional and available only with standard instrumentation. The Rally gauge cluster, which included an in-dash tachometer, didn't allow room for a clock in the gauge cluster. Pontiac had planned to release a second version of the Rally gauge cluster, which would have placed the tach on the hood and the other gauges in the dash, along with a clock. The second Rally gauge cluster was canceled before production began, although a few have been found in 1967 GTOs.

The luxurious interior appointments for a mid-sized car placed the GTO above many of its competitors in the musclecar field. Many buyers wanted a comfortable, mid-sized high-performance car, and the GTO suited their needs.

engine, right down to the 744 cam and stiff valve springs and dampers. Toward the end of the model year, the 670 cylinder head was replaced by the 97 head, which used a special set of valves and taller valve springs.

The Ram Air engine was offered only with 4.33:1 rear gears and was a real handful on the street. Put it on the drag strip in street trim and closed exhaust and The Great One could pull the quarter in 14.11 seconds at 100 mph. Breathe on it just a little by advancing the timing, loosening the belts and bolting on a set of cheaters and times would drop to 13.72 seconds. That was almost 0.5 second faster than the 1966 Tri-Power GTO.

Mated to the new 400 engine was a new transmission option, the three-speed Turbo Hydra-Matic, replacing the

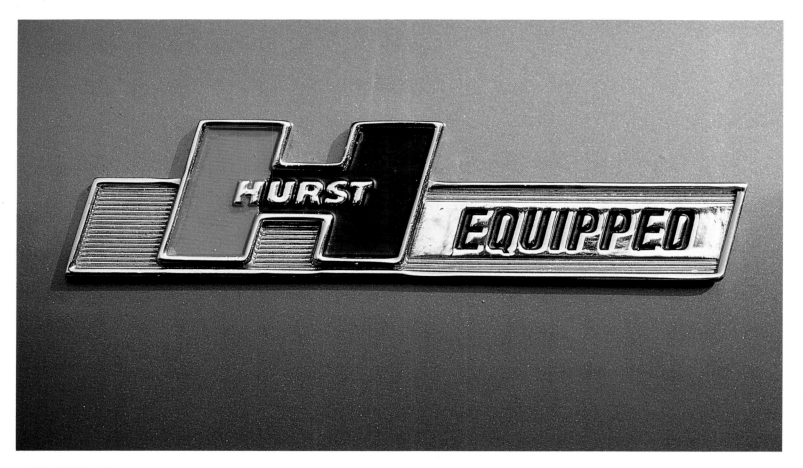

The Pontiac-Hurst relationship was still going strong in 1967. Although this plate was never installed by Pontiac on a GTO, many owners who purchased Hurst wheels or were just proud that their GTOs were equipped with Hurst shifters screwed a set of Hurst badges on their cars.

A solid-walnut gearshift knob was optional on the four-speed shifter only.

two-speed Powerglide that had been in use since 1964. The M40 Turbo Hydra-Matic was a strong, gutsy transmission that could handle the torque and shock of the powerful GTO engine. An automatic transmission was favored not only by the older, more sophisticated buyer, but also by the drag racer, who knew the automatic tranny would make him more consistent in the quarter mile.

When the console option was ordered with the Turbo Hydra-Matic, the Hurst Dual Gate shifter was standard equipment. Introduced in the early 1960s, the Dual Gate was picked up by Pontiac for use in 1967 as original equipment. The Dual Gate allowed the driver to leave the shifter in drive, permitting the transmission to shift at the factory's predetermined points. If he wanted to shift for himself, the driver slipped the lever into the right gate and slapped the lever forward. A positive latching mechanism prevented missed shifts, and it was virtually impossible to whack the lever into neutral and grenade the engine. Hurst claimed their new Dual Gate would "switch a lot of manual-shift lovers over to automatic." They were right. For the first time in GTO production history, automatic transmission-equipped models outsold the stick-shift versions by roughly 3,000 units.

The remainder of the drivetrain options and rear-axle ratios were essentially carried over from 1966, although the base three-speed manual transmission shift lever was moved from the steering column to the floor.

The exterior styling of the 1967 GTO was mostly unchanged from 1966, but cosmetic touchups were applied to the grilles, which received a handsome chrome mesh. The rocker panel was pulled up to cover the lower edge of the door, and the GTO emblem was dropped to the bottom of the fender and mounted in the bright rocker molding. A twin pinstripe highlighted the upper beltline. Around back, the bumper was redesigned, as was the trailing edge of the deck lid, providing a flat horizon across the rear. The taillamps were changed, now placed in two stacks of two on each side and recessed into the panel. The GTO nameplate remained in its usual location on the quarter panels and the deck lid.

Several new options appeared in 1967, including the Rally II wheel. The five-spoke wheel featured red lug nuts and a chrome-trimmed center cap with the letters PMD encased in a clear lens. The Rally wheel introduced in 1965 was still available, now designated Rally I. For improved stopping power, Delco Morraine front disc brakes were available. These four-piston units were offered with or without power assist.

Mechanically, there was little revision to the GTO's suspension or chassis in 1967. A relocated cross-member was used for the Turbo Hydra-Matic, and a new, dual-cylinder master brake system was standard equipment.

As always, every manual gearbox in 1967 GTOs was stirred by the famous Hurst shifter. The optional console was restyled in 1967 and had a woodgrained vinyl applique that matched the instrument panel fascia.

Wouldn't you know Hurst would introduce its new automatic control

wrapped in a '67 GTO?

It's only proper. Hurst has been in GTOs since the first GTO was born. Now that they've kicked loose the Great One for '67, with a new engine, drive train components and a 3-speed Turbo-Hydramatic, Hurst is in there with something new of its own. A console-mounted Dual Gate control that's going to switch a lot of manual-shift lovers over to automatic.

The reason is simple. Because the manual side of the Hurst automatic control is for *real*. This is no merchandising gimmick that promises you manual shift control, but in reality makes you guess your way through the automatic gears. The new Turbo-Hydro is a gutty, performance-prone transmission that's as home on a race track as it is on the highway. And controlling it can

be as precise as handling a fully synchronized manual transmission. The Dual Gate gives you that control with its positive latching mechanism that takes the guesswork out of gear-changing, going up or down. It eliminates any possibility of missing a gear, or accidentally hitting neutral and blowing an engine.

You're in complete control. You've got the automatic side when you feel shiftless and all the advantages of the manual side when you want to let it happen.

Soon you'll be able to buy Hurst automatic controls (along with all the other Hurst products) at your speed shop. Right now, though, you'll have to buy a Pontiac to get one. Write for details. Hurst Performance Products, Dept. 61C, Warminster, Pa. 18974.

HURST

34   CAR and DRIVER

Only 759 GTOs were equipped with the notchback bench seat and four-speed shifter. The Hurst T-handle was not standard equipment in 1967.

The GTO received a new transmission in 1967, the M40 Turbo Hydra-Matic, along with a new floorshifter for the M40, the Hurst Dual Gate. The Dual Gate, also known as the His and Hers, allowed the driver to either shift through the three-speed transmission or leave it in drive and let the transmission shift itself. It proved to be a popular option. For the first time, automatic transmission sales outstripped manual gearboxes. The stick-shift GTO would never outsell the automatic version again.

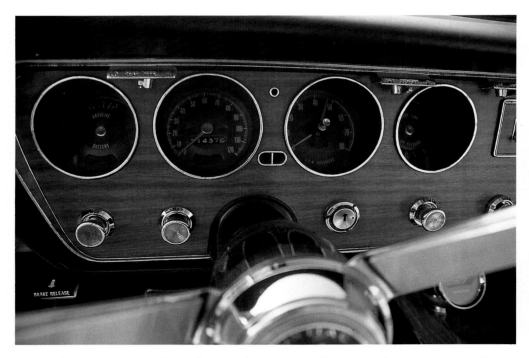

Few changes were made to the GTO's interior. The upholstery pattern was revised on seat and door panel surfaces, and a notchback bench seat was now offered at no extra cost. The dash pad was restyled, and a woodgrained plastic applique faced the instrument cluster fascia. The optional console was also covered in a woodgrained applique. The steering column was re-engineered to meet new federal safety regulations that required the column to collapse in a front-end collision, reducing the chance of injury to the driver. The standard steering wheel was a three-spoke design with a brushed-metal center cap and the horn buttons located in the spokes. Optional was the three-spoke Custom Sport wheel, unchanged from 1966 with the exception of a slightly revised horn bezel and cap.

Standard instrumentation was identical in appearance and placement for 1967. The Rally gauge cluster was again offered, and it too was a carbon copy of 1966; however, the oil pressure gauge was changed to peg at 80 psi, up from 60 psi in 1966.

Pontiac also released a new tachometer in 1967. Unlike most factory tachs, which were usually buried by the driver's knee or bolted to the console, this tach was right in the line of sight, mounted on the hood. This novel idea had been toyed with since 1965, and when released at the start of the 1967

The Rally gauge cluster was virtually unchanged from 1966 with the exception of an 80 lb. oil gauge.

Previous page
The rear styling was cleaned up for 1967. The taillamps were stacked four per side, and the deck line ran horizontally across the rear of the car.

The pancake-style air cleaner had first been introduced in 1965 and was continued through 1967. It was quite similar to the Corvette air cleaner.

model year, it was to be dealer installed only. Less than a month later, the hood-mounted tach became a regular production option and one of the most talked about new options in Detroit.

With sales of 81,722 units, The Great One held its own against the rising flood of competition in the marketplace. Only Lincoln and Cadillac weren't fielding some kind of musclecar in 1967. At Chrysler, both Plymouth and Dodge introduced their versions of the GTO. The Plymouth GTX carried the same basic dimensions as the GTO, and was powered by the 375 hp 440 ci engine. Dodge's entry was the Coronet R/T, also

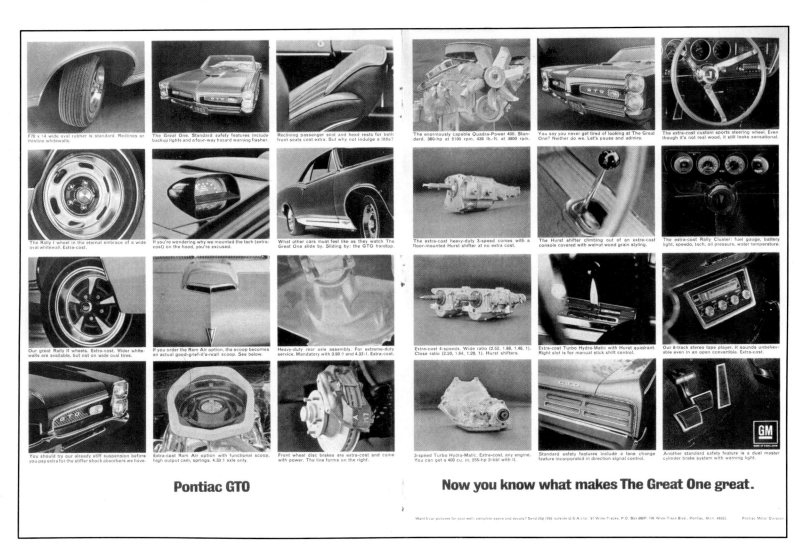

F70 x 14 wide oval rubber is standard. Redlines or thinline whitewalls.

The Great One. Standard safety features include backup lights and a four-way hazard warning flasher.

Reclining passenger seat and head rests for both front seats cost extra. But why not indulge a little?

The enormously capable Quadra-Power 400. Standard. 360-hp at 5100 rpm. 438 lb.-ft. at 3600 rpm.

You say you never get tired of looking at The Great One? Neither do we. Let's pause and admire.

The extra-cost custom sports steering wheel. Even though it's not real wood, it still looks sensational.

The Rally I wheel in the eternal embrace of a wide oval whitewall. Extra-cost.

If you're wondering why we mounted the tach (extra-cost) on the hood, you're excused.

What other cars must feel like as they watch The Great One slide by. Sliding by: the GTO hardtop.

The extra-cost heavy-duty 3-speed comes with a floor-mounted Hurst shifter at no extra cost.

The Hurst shifter climbing out of an extra-cost console covered with walnut wood grain styling.

The extra-cost Rally Cluster: fuel gauge, battery light, speedo, tach, oil pressure, water temperature.

Our great Rally II wheels. Extra-cost. Wider whitewalls are available, but not on wide oval tires.

If you order the Ram Air option, the scoop becomes an actual good-grief-it's-real! scoop. See below.

Heavy-duty rear axle assembly. For extreme-duty service. Mandatory with 3.90:1 and 4.33:1. Extra-cost.

Extra-cost 4-speeds. Wide ratio (2.52, 1.88, 1.46, 1). Close ratio (2.20, 1.64, 1.28, 1). Hurst shifters.

Extra-cost Turbo Hydra-Matic with Hurst quadrant. Right slot is for manual stick shift control.

Our 8-track stereo tape player. It sounds unbelievable even in an open convertible. Extra-cost.

You should try our already stiff suspension before you pay extra for the stiffer shock absorbers we have.

Extra-cost Ram Air option with functional scoop, high output cam, springs. 4.33:1 axle only.

Front wheel disc brakes are extra-cost and come with power. The line forms on the right.

3-speed Turbo Hydra-Matic. Extra-cost, any engine. You can get a 400 cu. in. 255-hp 2-bbl with it.

Standard safety features include a lane change feature incorporated in direction signal control.

Another standard safety feature is a dual master cylinder brake system with warning light.

Pontiac GTO

Now you know what makes The Great One great.

powered by the 375 hp 440. Both the GTX and the R/T could be powered by the 425 hp street Hemi. Chrysler was still a year away from finding the formula that would launch the success of the Pentastar performance program. The hardware was more than adequate, but Chrysler was to look long and hard at how Pontiac marketed the GTO and then apply those techniques with great success.

Ford continued their Fairlane GT and GTA, while Mercury stayed with the Cyclone GT. Both were basically unchanged, still powered by the 335 hp 390 engine and in a holding pattern until 1968, when they would be restyled and a new 428 ci engine would be offered in an attempt to make them more competitive with the GTO.

Corporate rivals Chevelle and Cutlass 4-4-2 grew stronger in 1967 as their programs initiated in 1965 came to market.

The SS396 Chevelle was the GTO's fiercest competitor, posting sales of 63,006 units, down from 72,272 in 1966. The 4-4-2 grew hair in 1967 with the addition of the W30 package, a cold-air package that included hand-selected engine parts, big cam with heavy-duty valve springs, fiberglass inner fenders and trunk-mounted battery. Rated at 360 hp, the W30 4-4-2 was a bruising, 13.8 second musclecar that was not kind to the GTO. Fortunately for Pontiac, it was a well-kept secret. Total 4-4-2 sales were 24,833 units, of which only a handful were W30s. The Buick Gran Sport trailed far behind, still lacking an image and an engine; sales were dismal at 13,813. It wouldn't be until 1970 that the 455 Stage 1 Gran Sport would gain a reputation as a torque monster.

The Great One also met new competition from within its own family. Pontiac fielded the Firebird, their own version of

Beginning in 1967, Pontiac changed the way they presented and sold the GTO. Corporate guidelines now forbade the use of action photography and other suggestions of aggressive driving. To counter these prohibitions, Jim Wangers assembled all the major components that made "The Great One great" into one two-page advertisement. The tiger of 1966 was quickly fading away.

Hurst wheels were offered in two finishes— gold and silver. Many Pontiac dealers would install Hurst wheels on new GTOs for their customers.

the Mustang-Camaro ponycar. The Firebird was offered in five different packages, using lessons learned from the GTO. The mild versions were powered by either a six-cylinder or a 326 V-8; however, two Firebirds were stepping on The Great One's shoes. Both were

The diecast GTO nameplates still appeared on the quarter panels. The upper beltline pinstripe now consisted of two paint lines.

The plastic grilles first introduced in 1966 were restyled. It was now a two-piece affair, with a handsome chrome mesh insert.

equipped with the 400 ci engine and both were rated at 325 hp, with one version equipped with Ram Air. The Firebird's horsepower figures were altered because the Firebird was 500 lb. lighter than the GTO, and although the F-bird's 400 was just as powerful as the heavier GTO, it was forbidden to break GM's policy of 1 hp for every 10 lb. of curb weight. There was another reason for underrating the Ram Air Firebird's horsepower rating, and it had to do with image. If the GTO was The Great One, flagship of the Pontiac performance fleet, it could not be outpowered by the new Firebird. On the street or strip, however, the 325 hp Firebird was capable of embarrassing its big brother.

Although the GTO faced increased competition, it retained a panache and style all its own, and that was the key to its continued strong sales. Other manufacturers screwed together high-performance cars that looked like GTOs

and ran like GTOs—but they weren't anything like the Pontiac GTO. Years later, Pontiac would field a GTO ad titled, "Others have caught on, but they haven't caught up." That ad was more than just advertising hype. It was a statement that rang true on the street, at the drive-ins and the drag strips across America. Dedicated men like Pete Estes, John DeLorean and Jim Wangers had poured their very souls into the GTO; it was one of the reasons no other car had its unique character.

Some of the strong styling cues that made the Pontiac GTO unmistakable on the road were the stacked vertical headlamps, the split-grille theme and the massive front bumpers.

Previous page
The 1967 GTO convertible in Signet Gold. The GTO grille nameplate featured chrome letters, filled with white paint and riding on a chrome bar. It was unchanged from 1964 to 1967.

The GTO's interior received only minor revisions for 1967. The instrument panel fascia was now covered in a woodgrained vinyl, the turn-signal indicator was split and the seat, door panel and quarter trim panel upholstery was restyled. Seatback locks were also new for 1967.

Red fender liners were first offered in 1966. Constructed of heavy-gauge plastic, the liners were molded to fit into the wheelhouses. The option was discontinued after 1967, since only 1,334 were sold on GTOs. The new five-spoke Rally II wheel was mounted on F70x14 in. redline tires. The styling for the new Rally II wheel was reminiscent of the Porsche road wheel, with its five cooling slots and recessed lug pockets.

The optional power antenna was available with both AM and AM-FM radios. It was mounted on the right-hand quarter panel.

Previous page
The 1967 GTO convertible in Tyrol Blue. In the second year of a two-year styling cycle, the 1967 GTO rode on a 115 in. wheelbase. The classic Pontiac styling cues of split grilles and Coke-bottle quarter-panel styling are evident.

Rear styling was simplistic, and that was part of its appeal. Pontiac had moved away from excessive trim, lots of chrome and other styling tricks. The functional looks set the GTO apart on the street.

The hood-mounted tachometer was a new option in 1967. Although it was first a dealer-installed option, within two months of production it became a factory-installed option.

It was lighted at night, controlled by the headlamps switch along with the instrument panel lamps.

Buying a 1967 GTO

The serious drag racer could put together a very competitive C/Stocker with the Ram Air GTO. If anything was working against the GTO, it was the price—assembling a hot Ram Air Goat resulted in a pretty stiff sticker. There was enough potential in the package, however, to build a street stocker that would go 12.4s, and in 1967, that was about 0.4 second *below* the NHRA C/Stock record.

Code	Description	Price
24207	GTO Sports Coupe	$3,029.00
75–	400 Ram Air Engine	263.30
781	Transmission, Three-Speed Automatic	226.44
731	Differential, Safe-T-Track, Heavy Duty	63.19
514	Fan—H.D. 7–Blade Fan and Clutch	3.05
584	Heater Deletion (Credit)	–71.76
681	Radiator—Heavy Duty	14.74
664	Regulator—Transistorized Voltage	10.53
634	Shocks—Super Lift Rear	39.50
671	Ignition—Capacitor Discharge System	104.26
622	Springs & Shocks—Heavy Duty	3.74
661	Frame–Heavy Duty	22.86
Total Price		$3,708.85

A drag racer ordering his 1967 GTO would do without options like a console or power accessories; they added weight, and weight is the enemy of the drag racer. Disc brakes also wouldn't be on the order sheet. They stop better, but they drag the wheels which slows the car. A Great One setup for the strip must also be a light one.

Production Figures

Production Figures by Body Style

Year	Body Style	Production
1964	Coupe	7,384
1964	Hardtop	18,422
1964	Convertible	6,644
Total		**32,450**
1965	Coupe	8,319
1965	Hardtop	55,722
1965	Convertible	11,311
Total		**75,352**
1966	Coupe	10,363
1966	Hardtop	73,785
1966	Convertible	12,798
Total		**96,946**
1967	Coupe	7,029
1967	Hardtop	65,176
1967	Convertible	9,517
Total		**81,722**

Production Figures by Transmission

Year	Transmission	Production
1964	Manual	NA
1964	Automatic	NA
1965	Manual	56,378
1965	Automatic	18,974
1966	Manual	61,279
1966	Automatic	35,667
1967	Manual	39,128
1967	Automatic	42,594

Production Figures by Engine

Year	Engine	Production
1964	389 3x2	8,245
1964	389 4bbl	24,205
1965	389 3x2	20,547
1965	389 4bbl	54,805
1966	389 3x2	19,045
1966	389 4bbl	77,901
1967	400 RA	751
1967	400 HO	13,827
1967	400 2bbl	2,967
1967	400 std	64,177

Production Figures for 1967 L67 Ram Air Engines

Block Code	Production
Manual	
XS	538
YR (California)	64
Total	**602**
Automatic	
XP	159
Total	**761***

Includes 10 service blocks.

Index